D1557609

FREE
TO
LEAD

THE DECISION-MAKING ETHOS OF HEALTHY GROWING CHURCHES

Rod Stafford

© 2011 by Rod Stafford
ISBN 978-0-61551-995-1

Published in Fairfax, VA by Rod Stafford.

Scripture quotations noted NIV are from the NEW INTERNATIONAL VERSION. © 1984, 2011 by Biblica, Inc. Used by permission. All rights reserved worldwide.

ISBN 978-0-61551-995-1

Library of Congress Cataloging-in-Publication Data

Stafford, Rod.
Free to Lead: The Decision-Making Ethos of Healthy Growing Churches / Rod Stafford

ISBN: 978-0-61551-995-1 (2011 Edition)
1. Church Leadership 2. Organizational Theory I. Title

Printed in the United States of America.

To my brother Gil
Friend, mentor, and role model
You showed me the power of good decision making

TABLE OF CONTENTS

ILLUSTRATIONS

ACKNOWLEDGEMENTS

No successful journey is made in isolation. It is always the product of community and that is certainly the case with this book. My heart is filled with a deep sense of gratitude for those who have helped me along the way.

I thank my late brother, Gil Stafford. Simply stated, this book would not have happened without him. This book was originally written as part of the Doctor of Ministry Studies Program at Anderson University School of Theology in candidacy for the degree of Doctor of Ministry. Gil convinced me to pursue a doctorate and encouraged me every step along the way. I was ready to quit on several occasions but he always asked the right questions and said the right things to keep me engaged. He wanted others to benefit from the Fairfax story and believed this project would help make that possible. My only regret is that he is not here to see the finished product. I miss him dearly.

I thank my wife, Donna. Much of the work for a project like this occurs in the time gaps between work and family life and can steal precious moments from both. Donna has been incredibly gracious about the time I have spent on this. She has cheered every book read, every interview completed, and every page written. I cannot count the times she has told me how proud she is of me. After thirty-one years of marriage, it still feels so good to hear those words.

I thank my Professional Development Team of Bob Moss and Joe Cookston. These two pastors and authors helped me to clarify and narrow the focus of this project and the end result is much better because of their input. Their genuine excitement for the topic convinced me that I was moving in the right direction. Their expertise in areas where I had little proved invaluable.

The same things can be said for my Local Support Team of Kathleen Otchy, Karen Kellogg, Jimmy Norris, Dennis Stotts, Mark Harmon, and David Black. This group, made up of staff members and board members, provided a source of real encouragement. A project like this takes away time from the things I get paid to do. They, however, not only gave me permission to pursue the project but cheered me on at every opportunity.

I thank my Executive Assistant, Valerie Dickson. Valerie arranged all of the interviews and surveys that this project required. She also became my data expert, not only helping to compile all of the data but figuring out how to present it in a clear and understandable fashion. I also thank Lainey Monroe for transcribing hours of recorded interviews so I could have easy access to the content.

I thank Elizabeth Hutchison and Mona Neff for being my editorial committee. Elizabeth made sure that my footnotes and bibliography would pass the Turabian test. Mona edited my project for grammar and sentence structure. I am almost embarrassed by how many editorial changes she suggested. I incorporated each one of them, however, and with each change the project was improved. What a gift.

I thank my Professional Project Committee of David Sebastian, Joe Cookston and Jerry Fox. Their thorough reading and thoughtful insights made this a much better project. Committees of this nature are often seen as obstacles to overcome but that was certainly not the case here. They were supportive and helpful in every way and were genuinely committed to my success.

I thank Mark Batterson, Marty Grubbs, Gideon Thompson, Steve Treash and Harry Kuehl for agreeing to be interviewed, speaking so candidly about their own journeys, giving me access to their staffs, and allowing me a glimpse into their decision-making ethos. I feel honored to be associated with each of these pastors and their congregations.

I thank Julie Falke who took on the responsibility of formatting the entire project so it could be published in book form. While I am extremely proud of the two bound copies of this professional project that now sit on the shelves of the Anderson University Library, what Julie produced is far more elegant and attractive.

Lastly, I thank Fairfax Community Church. This project reflects the twenty-four years I have been allowed to serve there. Their openness to take risks and their willingness to embrace change inspire me. They have loved me through each season of my life and my ministry. I have learned so much and am humbled by the opportunity to be called their pastor.

PREFACE

This book has been twenty-four years in the making. Twenty-four years ago I accepted a call to become the senior pastor of Fairfax Community Church. The invitation first came in the form of a phone call from Cecil Blackwell. At the time, I didn't know where Fairfax was located and when Cecil, who grew up Mississippi, said with a strong southern drawl that he was from Fairfax, Virginia, I imagined something very different than the teeming metropolitan area of Washington, D.C. That phone call began an incredible journey.

Donna and I moved from Anderson, Indiana to Fairfax in September of 1986. I was thirty years old and Donna was pregnant with our second child, Zach. Kora, our oldest, was four at the time. When I arrived in Fairfax, the church numbered about 100 people and was located on a dead-end street called Hunt Road. The congregation joked that it was appropriately named because people had to hunt to find the church. The location and size of the congregation, however, did not dampen their desire for genuine kingdom impact. There were organizational and structural barriers, which made that challenging but the congregation was open to change. Some of that change is chronicled in this book.

This book focuses on healthy decision making in local congregations. I have been a part of a local congregation my entire life. My father, D.C. Stafford, was a pastor for over sixty years. My brother, Gil Stafford, was in vocational ministry for fifty years as a pastor and a seminary professor. I entered vocational ministry when I was nineteen. When it comes to making decisions, I harbor no illusions that decision making in the local congregation is somehow easier because Christians are making the decisions. If anything, it may be more difficult. I know firsthand the frustration and heartache that occur when decision-making structures are unclear or the culture of decision making is unhealthy. My hope is that this book will serve as a helpful tool to enable local congregations to examine the way they make decisions and increase their kingdom impact in the world.

As mentioned earlier, this book was originally written as part of the Doctor of Ministry Studies Program at Anderson University School of Theology. I decided to maintain the same structure for this publication. Therefore, I have chosen to keep the chapter on methodology (Chapter 2) basically in tact. Those interested in the research process may find this chapter interesting. Others may want to go directly from Chapter 1 to Chapter 3 and refer back to this chapter as needed for background or clarification.

1 | The Importance of a Healthy Decision-Making Ethos

DECISIONS MATTER. THIS IS CERTAINLY TRUE ON A personal level. The decisions people make concerning relationships, education, vocation, personal behavior, and a myriad of other issues inevitably shape the course of their lives. The same is true for organizations. The decisions organizations make concerning what they do, why they do it, and how exactly they are going to accomplish it shape the future of the organization and impact its very existence. For Christians, the decisions made in local congregations should especially matter. If the local congregation plays a central role in God's kingdom activity, and I believe it does, then how and why decisions are made within the context of local congregations should be of significant interest to those who follow Christ.

My setting for ministry over the past twenty-four years has been Fairfax Community Church. I accepted the position of senior pastor right out of seminary. Though one

never really knows for certain where God's calling may
lead, I had a strong sense of God calling me to invest my
life in this one congregation, and to date, that has remained
the case. In those twenty-four years the congregation has
grown from 100 to over 2,000 in weekend worship attendance. This growth necessitated the ongoing evaluation of
systems and structures to ensure that inadequate or inap-
propriate processes did not negatively impact the mission
of the congregation. Over the years, the decision-making
ethos of the congregation emerged as a key issue. Change
was needed, but did not come easily.

When I arrived at Fairfax Community Church in 1986
the congregation utilized a decision-making structure that
is common in many smaller congregations. The Board of
Trustees held responsibility for finances and facilities, and
the Church Council was responsible for programming and
"spiritual" matters. The structure assumed that decisions
related to facilities and finances were not spiritual in nature
and that programming decisions did not involve facilities
and finances. In addition, numerous other committees
were responsible for various programs. The chairpersons
of each of those committees served on the Church Council
as an advocate for their particular area of ministry. Bylaws
formalized the structure, so changing it was cumbersome
at best.

The result was a lack of clarity concerning who really
"owned" decisions. By "owned" I refer not only to the
authority needed to make a decision but also to the responsibility and accountability for the decision made. It was

unclear who was entrusted with the authority to make a decision and who should be held responsible and accountable once the decision was made. If a decision needed to be made concerning Christian education, could the Christian Education Committee make it? Or did the Church Council need to make it because the decision involved programming and could potentially affect other programs? Or should the Board of Trustees decide because the issue involved the use of the facilities and had budget implications?

Additionally, what was the decision-making role of the senior pastor in all of this? When I first arrived at the church, certain members on the Board of Trustees questioned whether the pastor even needed to be present at meetings where decisions were made about facilities and finances. They assumed the pastor needed to be involved only in spiritual decisions. Thus, when I showed up at the first Board of Trustee meeting after my arrival, one member bluntly asked, "Why are *you* here?" In spite of the warm welcome, I stayed.

This lack of clarity in decision making resulted in frequent parallel conversations. Conversations would take place in a committee. Then the same conversation would take place in the Church Council. Then the same conversation would take place in the Board of Trustees. Each conversation involved a different group of people who would inevitably reframe the issue that needed to be decided. Often, this reframing of the decision would then start a whole new cycle of conversations.

As the church grew and staff was added, the number of

conversations needed to make a decision increased. Most decisions made at staff meetings were not real decisions. They had to run the gauntlet of committees and boards before they could be acted upon. The relationship of the staff to the various committees was even more vague and confusing. Was the staff person accountable to the committee or to the senior pastor? Did the youth pastor own decisions concerning youth ministry or did the Youth Council own those decisions? Were the various committees really ministry teams led by a staff person or were they responsible for governing a particular program or ministry? It was unclear, and since it was unclear, the default for most decisions was to involve as many people as possible to make sure all the bases were covered. This book is built on the assumption that my experience is not unique.

Decision-Making Ethos

In a general sense, the *ethos* of a community involves the guiding beliefs, values, or ideals that characterize the community. For the purpose of this book, the term ethos is used to describe the atmosphere or culture in which decisions are made within an organization. The decision-making ethos of an organization involves not only who is empowered to make certain decisions but also how those decisions are made. In this context, ethos concerns more than the decision-making structure of an organization. Structure focuses on the specificity of organizational charts, bylaws, policies, boards and committees. While ethos certainly influences structure, and structures can certainly restrict healthy decision making, ethos is not limited to a particular structure. It is possible for a similar decision-making ethos to be manifested in a number of different decision-making structures.

The current conversation concerning decision-making ethos in the church tends to juxtapose *hierarchical* and *collaborative* structures and prioritize one over the other. Hierarchical decision-making structures clearly define who in the organization is empowered to make certain decisions. There is a top and a bottom in the organization, and a clear line of authority runs between the two. Collaborative decision-making structures have no explicitly stated top or bottom. Decisions typically are entrusted to groups rather than individuals. The entire group or a subset of the group may make the decision. Specific skill sets or knowledge, rather than position in the organization, usually determine whose voice is most dominant in a particular decision.

This book hopes to suggest that there exists a third way of organizational decision making that is best described by the term *collaborative hierarchy*.

> Simply stated, collaborative hierarchy provides clarity concerning the ultimate ownership of a decision based on positional authority within the hierarchy, but encourages the decision-maker to invite others into the conversation, regardless of position in the hierarchy, for the purpose of making the best

decision possible. In a collaborative
hierarchy, positional authority is most
profoundly demonstrated in the freedom
of the decision-maker to determine
who is brought into the conversation.

State of the Church in America

The importance of addressing the issue of healthy
decision making in the context of the local congregation
has never been greater. Many pastors struggle with issues
related to decision making. Cumbersome or unclear decision-making structures can have a debilitating effect on
the ability of a congregation to engage the culture with the
good news of the kingdom and often results in underuti-
lization of kingdom resources.

In his book, *The American Church in Crisis*, David T.
Olson deals with the current state of the church in the United
States. While roughly 40 percent of Americans report that
they regularly attend church, data compiled in 2004 from
more than 300,000 Christian congregations in the United
States found that those churches totaled only about 52
million in attendance. This represented 17.7 percent of the
American population in 2004.[1] According to these statis-
tics, the church in the United States is losing ground to
the growth of the population at an alarming rate. In just
under forty years, the United States population expanded
by 100 million people. From 1967 to 2006 it grew from

200 million to 300 million.[2] The church, however, failed to keep up with even this very modest rate of growth. From 1990 to 2006 church attendance remained virtually unchanged at around 52 million people. The net result is that church attendance as a percentage of the population fell from 20.4 percent to 17.5 percent during this period. If the church in the United States continues its current trends, the percentage of people attending worship will decline from 17.5 percent to 14.7 percent by 2020.[3]

While the factors contributing to this decline are complex, the decision-making ethos of the church must be included in the discussion. The missional momentum that allows churches to grow and reproduce requires a healthy decision-making ethos. Many congregations employ a decision-making ethos that makes it difficult to gain the momentum necessary to either reproduce themselves through church planting or to restructure the ministry of the church for missional success. Change is often arduous and slow. Leaders spend a tremendous amount of energy on issues that do little to advance the missional agenda of the church. Systemic issues make it difficult for the ministry of the church to align with the message of the church. The idea that any decision-making structure can work as long as "good people" are a part of it is naïve and coun-ter-productive. Many churches are filled with good people laboring in structures that create unnecessary conflict and ambiguity over even the most routine decisions. Conflicts arise based not on what decisions are being made but on who is empowered to make them.

A Leadership Drain

More and more, duly appointed leaders find themselves unable to effectively lead. The church landscape is littered with gifted, highly capable leaders who exited pastoral ministry because they tried to carry out the radical agenda of the kingdom in a structure that simply was not suited for anything radical. Some gave up on vocational ministry altogether, while others found avenues to express their kingdom passions outside of the local congregation. Many young, emerging Christian leaders, tired of fighting committees and boards over visional and operational issues, simply decided to go to an organization (or start an organization) where they could lead effectively. The resulting leadership drain has impacted the ability of local congregations to remain on the forefront of kingdom advancing activity.

Minimalist Organizations

The crisis in which the American church finds itself is sometimes minimized because of the low mortality rates of congregations. The closure rate of congregations from 1998 to 2005 was 1 percent. This represents a closure rate much lower than businesses and other non-profit organizations.[4] Shauna L. Anderson, in an article entitled, *Dearly Departed—How Often Do Congregations Close*, suggests that the reason congregations have such low mortality rates compared to other organizational populations is not reflective of stronger organizational strength but the ability of congregations to "limp along" in a weakened state for longer periods of time than other organizations.[5] She refers to these weakened congregations as "minimalist organizations."[6]

In the midst of difficult times, congregations can drastically reduce activity and still remain open. Most other organizations cannot survive in this weakened state. This condition is not exclusive to small congregations. Many highly successful, rapidly growing churches of the past twenty or thirty years are no longer thriving congregations. While they continue to exist, probably for many years, they have lost their momentum and missional edge. New pastors may come and go, but the best days of the church remain in the past.

This ability to survive in such a weakened state usually creates conflict between those in the congregation who favor change that will move the congregation toward missional success and those who prefer the status quo. The decision-making ethos of the congregation often determines the outcome of that conflict. If the decision-making ethos empowers those in the congregation who favor the status quo, then the congregation will continue to function in its weakened state. The result is human and financial resources that could be leveraged for kingdom impact are, in effect, frozen. Unfortunately, this describes a significant number of churches in the United States. Olsen states, "If trends continue, by 2050 the percentage of Americans attending church will be half the 1990 figure."[7]

The revitalization of these weakened congregations is often pursued without addressing the underlying decision-making structure of the church. No amount of conferences or outreach programs or visioning conferences will help if the local congregation continues a decision-making ethos that is unhealthy and unclear. The result is the misuse of even greater amounts of human and financial capital.

The Importance of Cities

This book examines the decision-making ethos of six large, multi-staff congregations that have grown over a long period of time and are located in metropolitan areas. The focus on metropolitan areas reflects the growing importance of cities in the missional activity of the church. A dramatic population shift from rural to urban and suburban settings took place over the past century. According to the Census Bureau, "'metropolitanization' particularly characterized the demographic change of the United States in the twentieth century. Prior to World War II, the majority of Americans lived outside of metropolitan territory. By the end of the century, four out of every five people in the United States resided in a metropolitan area."[8] This population shift was consistent and unrelenting as reflected in the fact that, "the U.S. population grew increasingly metropolitan each decade, from 28 percent in 1910 to 80 percent in 2000."[9] In addition, "eight states—California, Connecticut, Florida, Maryland, Massachusetts, New Jersey, New York, and Rhode Island—had all reached at least 90 percent metropolitan population by 2000."[10]

Metropolitan areas of all sizes experienced significant growth. The greatest concentration of growth, however, occurred in larger metropolitan areas. In fact, "[s]ince 1990, more than half of the U.S. population has lived in metro-politan areas of at least one million people."[11] According to the Census Bureau, total U.S. population in 2000 was 281 million. That same year, the ten largest metropolitan areas: New York, Los Angeles, Chicago, Washington-Baltimore, San Francisco-Oakland, Philadelphia, Boston, Detroit, Dallas-Fort Worth, and Houston had a combined population of over 88 million.[12] Nearly one-third of the entire population of the United States resided in just ten cities.

Global Shift

The population shift in the United States reflects a global shift taking place from rural to metropolitan areas. Demographers watching urban trends marked 2007 as the year when the world entered a new urban millennium in which the majority of its people now live in cities.[13] The rate of growth of these world cities has been breathtaking.

> In 1950 New York and London were the only world cities with metro-area populations of over 10 million people. Today, however, there are more than twenty such cities—twelve of which achieved that ranking in the last two decades with many more to come. World cities are becoming more and more economically and cultur-

ally powerful; cities are the seats of
multinational corporations and international economic, social, and technological networks. The technology/communi-
cation revolution means that the culture
and values of global cities are now being
transmitted around the globe to every
tongue, tribe, people, and nation. Kids in
Iowa or even Mexico are becoming more
like young adults in Los Angeles and New
York City than they are like adults in their
own locales. The coming world order will
be a global, multicultural, urban order.
World cities are increasingly crucial in
setting the course of culture and life as
a whole even in areas of the world, such
as Europe and North America, where
cities are not literally growing in size.[14]

Cities are magnets for every religion, philosophy, cult,
and movement in the world. In business terms, the church
has lost an alarming amount of "market share" in some of
the largest, most influential cities of the world. The church is
no longer on the cutting edge of influence. Other religions,
philosophies, and cults are capturing the hearts and minds
of those who live in these great cities. This impacts not only
individual values but also the entire culture.

Gateway Cities

A first-century world has emerged in the twenty-first
century. In the first century, the apostle Paul faced a plural-

istic religious landscape where there was no consensus on the important issues of life—the nature of God, salvation, eternal life, or truth. How did Paul effectively spread the good news of Jesus Christ in this pluralistic environment? Under the leadership of the Holy Spirit, Paul targeted large, globally connected cities. These *gateway* cities, like Ephesus, Corinth, and Rome were central to God's mission to "make disciples of all nations." Those who came to Christ in these cities were highly mobile and influential. These cities literally became the gateway for the spread of the gospel to "the ends of the earth." Now "the ends of the earth" have come to the cities. People from every tribe, tongue, and nation reside in these teeming metropolitan areas. Gateway cities have once again become the strategic focal point for the spread of the gospel in the twenty-first century.

Dr. Tim Keller, pastor of Redeemer Presbyterian Church in New York City, recently addressed the 2010 Lausanne Conference in Cape Town, South Africa. He focused on the importance of cities in the global spread of the gospel. He points out that cities have been an integral part of the mission of the church from the beginning.

> The church lives as an international, dispersed fellowship of congregations, as Israel did under the exile. In Acts 8, we see God forcibly dispersing the Christians from Jerusalem, thus boosting Christian mission enormously. They immediately went to Samaria, a city that Jewish people would have been taught

> to despise as much as Jonah despised
> Nineveh or the Jews despised Babylon.
> But unlike the reluctant prophet or
> exiles, the gospel-changed Christians
> made them immediately effective in
> urban mission in Samaria (Acts 8:1ff).[15]

Keller goes on to point out that as the gospel spread, the importance of cities grew beyond any particular city to cities in general.

> In Acts 17, Paul goes to Athens, the *intel-
> lectual* center of the Greco-Roman world.
> In Acts 18, he travels to Corinth, one of
> the *commercial* centers of the empire. In
> Acts 19, he arrives in Ephesus, perhaps
> the Roman world's *religious* center as the
> hub of many pagan cults and particularly
> of the imperial cult, with three temples
> for emperor worship. By the end of Acts,
> Paul makes it to Rome, the empire's
> *power* capital, the military and political
> center of that world. John Stott concludes:
> "It seems to have been Paul's deliberate
> policy to move purposefully from one
> strategic city-centre to the next." If the
> gospel is unfolded at the urban center,
> you reach the region and the society.[16]

Healthy, Growing Congregations

While some may say the church has been slow to respond to this seismic shift in population, an increasing number of healthy, growing "megachurches" are located in these gateway cities. The term "megachurch" generally refers to Protestant congregations with an average weekend worship attendance of at least 2,000. Recent data indicates that "there are 1,210 Protestant churches in the United States with weekly attendance over 2,000, nearly double the number that existed five years ago."[17] In terms of location, these "megachurches are concentrated around the largest cities."[18] Megachurches, as well as other large, growing congregations that may not meet the megachurch criteria, require considerable-sized staffs to mobilize people for ministry and accomplish their mission. The speed and frequency with which decisions must be made often characterizes these congregations. The decision-making ethos can either inhibit or enhance missional effectiveness.

In 2007 the number of megachurches in the United States had increased 108 percent over the 2000 figures. While representing less than one-half of one percent of all churches in the United States, the attendance at these churches is approximately 4.5 million.[19] In their book, *Beyond Megachurch Myths: What We Can Learn from America's Largest Churches*, Scott Thumma and Dave Travis make the case that this rapid growth of megachurches is not a fad that will soon come to an end, but rather is linked to organizational changes taking place in American society. As Americans have grown increasingly comfortable interacting with large stores, large businesses, large cities and large organizations, they have also become comfortable in very large churches. This phenomenon seems less tied to the boomer generation and more a reflection of macro trends within culture.[20] In fact, the average age of attendees in megachurches is significantly lower than in smaller churches. In addition, churches focused on reaching the next generation for Christ have fueled the rapid growth in the number of megachurches over the last seven years.[21] While some may mourn the impact of large institutions on our culture, these institutions reflect a powerful, and seemingly lasting, trend. As long as large institutions remain a significant part of our culture, the attractiveness of very large churches will remain.

This reality means that understanding the decision-making ethos of larger congregations is of paramount importance. Thumma and Travis believe that one of the key factors in the growth and sustainability of megachurches is the speed with which these congregations can respond to changing trends within the culture.[22] Their decision-making ethos allows for significant change to take place in a relatively short period of time. This nimbleness in making decisions, even in such a large organization, appears to be a reflection of hierarchical clarity. However, in settings where there is uncertainty concerning who is empowered to make decisions, then successfully navigating change becomes increasingly difficult.

Chapter Summary

Decisions matter. For Christians, the decisions made in local congregations should especially matter. This book looks at a decision-making ethos that is best described as *collaborative hierarchy*. For the purpose of this book, the term ethos describes the atmosphere or culture in which decisions are made in an organization. Collaborative hierarchy provides clarity concerning the ultimate ownership of a decision based on positional authority within the hierarchy, but encourages the decision-maker to invite others into the conversation, regardless of position in the hierarchy, for the purpose of making the best decision possible.

A dramatic population shift from rural to urban and suburban settings took place over the last century, increasing the importance of cities in the mission of the church. These *gateway* cities are a strategic focal point for the spread of the gospel in the twenty-first century. This population shift coincides with the growth of very large congregations, many of which are located in these cities. These healthy, growing congregations require a decision-making ethos that is nimble enough to respond effectively to the mission opportunities that arise in a rapidly changing culture.

2 | Methodology

THE RESEARCH FOR THIS BOOK INCLUDES A COMBINA-
tion of interviewer-administered questionnaires and
self-completion surveys. The interviews were with five
senior pastors of large, growing congregations. The surveys
were given to the staff of those same five congregations.
In addition, the staff of Fairfax Community Church where
I currently serve as the senior pastor was also surveyed.
The interviews and surveys explored the decision-making
ethos of each congregation. The research also includes a
brief review of key biblical passages that allow the reader
to observe a decision-making ethos reflected both in Old
Testament Israel and in the New Testament church. Additionally, it includes the integration of contemporary literature pertaining to the decision-making ethos of organizations
in general and congregations specifically. What immediately
follows is a more detailed explanation of the process and
rationale for the interviews and surveys utilized in this book.

Congregational Selection

This book focuses on healthy, growing churches that are located in large metropolitan areas. Specifically, it examines six congregations that have experienced an average annual growth rate in weekend worship services of at least 10 percent a year over a period of ten years and are located in U.S. metropolitan areas of more than one million. In addition, the current senior pastor has served at the church for a minimum of ten years.[1]

Focusing on congregations that demonstrated healthy growth over a sustained period of time lessens the likelihood that the growth of the congregation results from some singular event in the life of the church. Many factors can affect the growth of a congregation. The longer the period of sustained growth, the less likely that growth is to be related to a single event and the more likely it is to be related to something within the culture of the congregation.

Focusing on congregations where the senior pastor has been at the church for an extended period of time resulted in two benefits. It provided a consistent voice that could reflect on the journey the congregation has been on in the area of decision making. It also increased the likelihood that the general philosophy concerning decision making had not changed drastically during the growth of the congregation. The six congregations are Black Rock Congregational Church, National Community Church, The Church at Rancho Bernardo, Crossings Community

Church, Jubilee Christian Church, and Fairfax Community Church.

Steve Treash is the senior pastor at Black Rock Congregational Church. Established over 150 years ago, Black Rock is a non-denominational church located in Fairfield, Connecticut, just outside New York City. Treash grew up in the Chicago area. He moved to Connecticut when he was a junior in high school and started attending Black Rock. In 1987, after graduating from seminary, Black Rock called Treash to be its associate pastor. He served in that role for ten years and then became the senior pastor in 1997. He has been in that role for the past thirteen years.[2] When Treash became the senior pastor of Black Rock, average weekend worship attendance was 700. Over the past thirteen years, Black Rock has grown to over 2,000 in average weekend worship attendance in six weekend services utilizing two campuses.[3]

Mark Batterson is the senior pastor at National Community Church in Washington, D.C. National Community Church is an interdenominational church that is strategically aligned with several organizations: the Assemblies of God, the Association of Related Churches, the Willow Creek Association and the Mosaic Alliance.[4] Batterson started the church in 1996 with twenty-five people. They now average over 2,000 people in their weekend worship services. National Community Church is a multi-site fellowship that meets in both rented and permanent facilities for worship services and church events. Presently, they meet in six locations in the metro

D.C. area.

Harry Kuehl is the senior pastor of the Church at Rancho Bernardo. Located in the San Diego metro area, the congregation is affiliated with the Church of God (Anderson, IN). Kuehl and his wife Candace, along with another couple, started the church in 1990. From its four original members the congregation has now grown to a worshipping community of 2,000 in three weekend services, all which take place at one location.[5] Prior to pastoring the Church at Rancho Bernardo, Kuehl was the senior pastor at another church located in the San Diego area.

Marty Grubbs is the senior pastor at Crossings Community Church in Oklahoma City. Crossings Community was established in 1959 and is affiliated with the Church of God (Anderson, IN). Grubbs initially was called to be the associate pastor at the church. He served in that role for several years and then became the senior pastor in 1985. At the time the church averaged just over 150 in weekend worship attendance.[6] Over the next twenty-five years the church grew to an average worship attendance of over 4,500 in six weekend services located in three different settings on its large suburban campus.[7]

Bishop Gideon Thompson is the senior pastor of Jubilee Christian Church. The congregation is located in Boston and is affiliated with the Church of God (Anderson, IN). Thompson started the church in 1982 after resigning from another congregation he had pastored for ten years, also located in the Boston metro area. Over the past twenty-eight years the congregation has grown to over 6,000 in weekend worship attendance.[8] The congregation has five weekend worship services spread between two campuses.

For the past twenty-five years I have had the honor of being the senior pastor of Fairfax Community Church. Fairfax Community Church is located in metropolitan Washington D.C., just west of downtown in Fairfax County, Virginia. The church was started in 1929 and is affiliated with the Church of God (Anderson, IN). Upon graduating seminary, I came to the congregation in 1986. At that time, the congregation averaged 100 in weekend worship attendance. Over the past twenty-four years it has grown to over 2,000 in average weekend worship attendance in four services at one location.

Interviews

The senior pastor of each of the other five churches surveyed completed an interviewer-administered questionnaire. The interviews consisted of questions focused on changes that have taken place in the way decisions are made in their particular congregation, how collaboration is fostered, what struggles that have been faced, how ownership of decisions is determined, how vision is formed, and what advice they would give to other congregational leaders concerning decision making. (Appendix 1) The interviews provided a broader narrative and a helpful context for the data received from the staff surveys.

Survey

Verbal consent was acquired from each participating senior pastor to survey the staff of the congregation that they lead. Senior pastors were given the freedom to choose which staff would be asked to participate in the survey. The survey measured the degree to which the decision-making ethos of each staff member's particular congregation was hierarchical and the degree to which it was collaborative. (Appendix 2) The two positions were not pitted against each other. In other words, answers that indicated the decision-making ethos of the congregation was very hierarchical did not automatically mean that the decision-making ethos was not collaborative. The reverse was true as well. Answers that indicated a high degree of collaboration did not automatically mean the decision-making ethos was not hierarchical.

A numerical value was assigned to each answer. A graph was then designed consisting of a collaborative and hierarchy axis. Each axis runs from 1 (the lowest score possible) to 5 (the highest score possible). The graph was then divided into four quadrants. On the collaborative axis, any score above 3 was considered high collaborative and any score below 3 was considered low collaborative. Likewise, on the hierarchy axis, any score above 3 was considered high hierarchy and any score below 3 was considered low hierarchy.

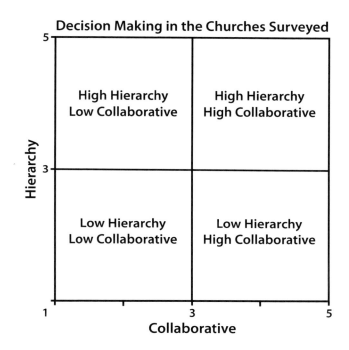

Illustration 1. Collaborative Hierarchy - Four-pane graph

By plotting the two scores of each respondent along the collaborative and hierarchy axis, it is possible to visualize the degree to which each individual surveyed views the decision-making ethos of their congregation as hierarchical and the degree to which they view it as collaborative. Responses were anonymous, but each respondent was asked to indicate his or her gender and age. This provided the means to observe whether there were significant differences in the responses based on gender or age demographic. As shown in the graph, there are four possible outcomes for each person who took the survey.

1. Low Hierarchy/Low Collaborative – This reflects a decision-making ethos that demonstrates very little hierarchy and at the same time demonstrates very little collaboration. The organization would be very flat structurally with little positional leadership, yet decisions would often be made in an isolated fashion with little or no input from others in the organization.

2. Low Hierarchy/High Collaborative – This reflects a decision-making ethos that demonstrates very little hierarchy but a great deal of collaboration. The organization would be flat structurally with little positional leadership but would engage in a great deal of dialogue across the breadth of the organization in making decisions.

3. High Hierarchy/Low Collaborative – This reflects a decision-making ethos that demonstrates a high degree of hierarchy but very little collaboration. The organization would have clear lines of authority and clearly designated leaders based on position in the organization who are empowered to make decisions, but decisions would often be made in an isolated fashion with little or no input from others in the organization.

4. High Hierarchy/High Collaborative – This reflects a decision-making ethos that demonstrates a high degree of hierarchy and also a high degree of collaboration. The organization would have clear

lines of authority and clearly designated leaders based on position in the organization who are empowered to make decisions, and at the same time would engage in a great deal of dialogue across the breadth of the organization in making decisions.

Delimitations

This book focuses on the decision making that takes place within the local congregation. It concentrates on large visional decisions that determine congregational direction and heading and on day-to-day decisions that must be made in order to implement that vision. The focus is not on broader denominational structures in which congregations exist. There may be principles that apply to broader denominational structures, and to organizations in general, but that is not the subject of this book.

This book looks at congregations that have experienced consistent growth over a sustained period of time. The focus is on discovering what best describes their decision-making ethos. The book does not assume that if a church adopts the decision-making ethos of these congregations, it will automatically experience a similar rate of growth. Many factors contribute to the growth of a congregation, and decision-making ethos is only one variable. However, the book does suggest that healthy congregations that have experienced consistent growth over a sustained period of time may very well reflect a decision-making ethos similar to these six congregations.

The idea of church growth has fallen out of favor in recent years. It was probably overemphasized in the past few decades. It is probably underemphasized now. This book is built on the assumption that growth in the attendance of the weekend worship of a local congregation is a positive. The book does not argue that attendance growth is of singular importance or of paramount importance, only that, given the alternative, it is a positive. There seems to be no compelling argument for why congregation attendance decline is positive and worthy of pursuit. The rapid growth of the Jerusalem church from a congregation of a 120 to a congregation that numbered in the thousands seems to at least hint at the possibility of a connectedness between missional success and congregational growth.

Equally important to note is that the scope of this book does not include the role the Holy Spirit plays in decision making. It is assumed that all decisions that are made within the local congregation should be made within the context of God's will and reflect God's guidance. The role of prayer and scripture in the life of the decision-maker is not directly addressed but is certainly understood. Prayer and scripture can be, and often are, utilized in widely divergent decision-making structures. The focus of this book is the decision-making ethos out of which godly discernment takes place.

Goal

The goal of this book is to provide pastors and congregational leaders a helpful framework for looking at decision making in their own congregations. By providing a framework that is informed by the biblical narrative as well as the experience of other organizations in general and healthy, growing congregations specifically, pastors will have an additional tool for developing a healthy decision-making ethos in which ministry can flourish. This may also position the congregation to be more attractive to strong, visionary leadership and allow the congregation to better navigate the change required to steward its human and financial resources for missional success.

Pastors or congregational leaders are so invested in a particular way of functioning that they may not be aware of weaknesses that are present in their decision-making ethos or how improvements might be made. This book offers congregations an additional tool in determining the decision-making ethos that is best for their congregation.

Target Audience

This book is written to two primary audiences. First, it is written to those who may view hierarchy as one of the problems in the twenty-first century church. The book examines biblical and practical examples of hierarchy, the importance and role of hierarchy, and its potential misuse. Secondly, it is written to those who understand the impor-

tance of hierarchy but may not fully understand the power
and purpose of collaboration. It is written to those who
may confuse consensus with collaboration and in rejecting
the former have missed out on the rich leadership value of
the latter.

Collaboration unleashes the full potential of hierarchy.
Without collaboration, hierarchy becomes a rigid system
that maintains organizational integrity but misses the
dynamism that healthy organizations possess. Without
hierarchy, collaboration results in an unofficial and often
unspoken territorialism where the sands of the decision-
making ethos of the congregation are ever shifting and
there is a constant churn over who is entrusted with what
decision. This positioning for congregational influence
is always masked behind religious jargon and "Christian
smiles," but it is often a vicious battle.

Chapter Summary

The research for the book includes a combination of
interviewer-administered questionnaires and self-completion surveys that explore the decision-making ethos of six
congregations that have experienced an average annual
growth rate in weekend worship services of at least 10
percent per year over a period of ten years, are located in
U.S. metropolitan areas of over one million, and the current
senior pastor has been at the church for a minimum of ten
years. The interviews consisted of questions that focused
on the current decision-making ethos of each congrega-

tion and changes that have taken place over the years. The survey measured the degree to which the decision-making ethos of each staff member's particular congregation was hierarchical and the degree to which it was collaborative. The research for this book also includes a review of key biblical passages and contemporary literature pertaining to decision making.

3 | The Case for Hierarchy

THE STAFFS OF THE SIX CONGREGATIONS THAT WERE the focus of this book were asked to complete a survey regarding the decision-making ethos of the congregation in which they serve. The survey was designed to measure the degree to which the decision-making ethos of their particular congregation was hierarchical and the degree to which it was collaborative. On the hierarchical scale, the results could range from almost no degree of hierarchy (1) to extremely hierarchical (5). The following graph shows that all but four of the seventy-three persons surveyed scored in the high hierarchy quadrant. Three scored exactly in the middle between high hierarchy and low hierarchy, and one scored in the low hierarchy quadrant (next page).

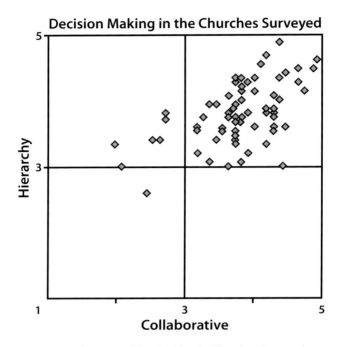

Illustration 2. Decision Making in Churches Surveyed

Growth and Hierarchy

The results of the survey seem to be supported by the interviews with the senior pastors of each congregation. Mark Batterson started National Community Church in 1996 with twenty-five people. They now average over 2,000 people in their weekend worship services. Batterson says that, initially, the decision-making ethos of the church was quite simple. He says, "I used to do everything and make all of the decisions."[1] However, that changed as the church began to grow and the demands of ministry increased. He goes on to say, "I remember the moment, seven to eight years in, when a staff member came and asked me whether we should get a 75-watt light bulb or a 100- watt light bulb. I thought, 'Oh boy!' After that I became very proactive in delegating decisions. As the church has grown, I'm micromanaging a lot less and delegating decisions a lot more. The staff members know they are empowered to make decisions."[2]

Marty Grubbs, senior pastor at Crossings Community Church in Oklahoma City, has a similar journey. Grubbs became the pastor of Crossings Community Church in 1985. At the time the church averaged just over 150 in weekend worship attendance. Over the next twenty-five years the church grew to an average worship attendance of over 4,500 in six weekend services. Grubbs says that the growth of this large congregation changed the way in which decisions are made. He says, "I make fewer decisions now than when the church was smaller. However, the decisions I make seem much heavier, and they're more strategic to the vision than they ever were. In the early days, my decision making was much more operational in nature. Now, other people are making those decisions."[3]

Batterson's and Grubb's commitment to delegation in a growing organization is not an unusual journey. Anyone who has started a small business or a non-profit or a congregation understands the need to delegate as the organization grows. Delegation, however, is the product of hierarchy. Clarity concerning who has the authority to make a particular decision allows delegation to take place.

Individuals cannot delegate to others what they are not already empowered to do. A hierarchical structure helps to clarify who is entrusted with what decisions.

Bishop Gideon Thompson started Jubilee Christian Church in 1982. Over the past twenty-eight years, the congregation has grown to over 6,000 in weekend worship attendance. Thompson describes the process of developing a healthy decision-making ethos in a new church, "When we started, there were no organizational obstacles to overcome. The people who were initially attracted to the church didn't have any organizational model they were trying to force us into. We had an opportunity to slowly structure the ministry as we prayed, sought the Lord, and asked other brethren."[4] Hierarchical structure and clear lines of authority and accountability have been a part of its ethos from the beginning. Thompson points out that this includes the accountability of the senior pastor: "I'm a bishop and I'm under Bishop Garlington, who pastors Covenant Church of Pittsburgh. While I believe it's important for the head of a ministry to have the authority to project the vision and the direction of that ministry, that person who has authority needs to also be under authority."[5]

Harry Kuehl started the Church at Rancho Bernardo in 1990. From its four original members the congregation has now grown to a worshipping community of 2,000. Kuehl describes the changes that occurred over the past twenty years in terms of the decision-making ethos of the church, "There is an evolution of leadership style that's occurred in our church." Before Kuehl launched the church, there was only a small Bible study. Kuehl describes the changes that began to take place structurally when that small group became interested in launching a church, "We immediately formed a leadership team. Eventually, as the church grew, we went to an elder board structure. That was a big decision because it placed all of the pastors underneath their authority."[6] Kuehl's experience is not an isolated one. As long as only a few people are involved in an organization or community, the need for hierarchical clarity does not seem particularly pressing. However, as an organization grows, there is a need for increased clarity in areas of authority, accountability, and decision making.

Fuzzy Hierarchy

Many congregations have, what might best be called, a "fuzzy" hierarchy. In this context, fuzzy hierarchy refers to the belief that there should be some level of authority and accountability in the decision-making structure of the congregation, but it is unclear how that structure is intended to function. For instance, many congregations believe that congregational members should somehow be involved in making decisions. But the way they should be involved is often unclear. Is their involvement in decision making best manifested in the form of congregational business meetings and votes? Is it best manifested in the form of boards and committees, where decisions are owned by a particular group? Or is it best manifested in some other way? Much of the decision-making conflict that occurs in congregations focuses on *who* is empowered to make the decision rather than *what* decision is actually made.

Black Rock Congregational Church provides a helpful example of a congregation that was able to move from a fuzzy hierarchy to a hierarchy with a great deal more clarity. When Steve Treash became the senior pastor of Black Rock, the average weekend worship attendance was 700. Over the past thirteen years, Black Rock has grown to over 2,000 in weekend worship attendance.

When Treash first assumed the role of senior pastor, the decision-making ethos of the church did, to a great degree, reflect a fuzzy hierarchy. Treash explains the structure he inherited and some of the changes that have taken place over the past thirteen years, "What I inherited was a model where the senior pastor was viewed as one rather small link in a decision chain. That decision chain was primarily a mixture of staff decision making and board decision making. Each ministry had a board, and as the church grew, there was a staff person connected to each board." The result was a situation where it was unclear who had the authority to make decisions. He continues, "Sometimes the board felt like they had an oversight role over the staff person. Sometimes the staff person was a stronger personality and used the board as a ministry team. There were all sorts of opportunities for hurt feelings because decisions would be made that the board thought they should vote on and the staff person did not."[7]

Over the years, changes were made in the decision-making ethos of the congregation. Now there is a relationship between the staff and the Elder Board that Treash describes as "staff directed and elder protected." The result is a great deal more clarity in decision making. He reports, "There's a clearer relationship now between the staff and the boards. All staff members have supervisors within the staff. The senior staff reports to the Elder Board. We've cleared up the decision-making process considerably."[8]

Role of the Board

John Carver is passionate about the ability of organizations to accomplish the mission around which they were formed. He recognizes that this is often hindered by a fuzzy hierarchy, particularly when it comes to the way in which the governing board of an organization functions. The lack of clarity in board responsibility and function has thwarted the missional success of many organizations. Carver's particular focus is on nonprofit organizations. He has developed a model for how boards can function at their best that has become known as "The Carver Model," which clarifies board functionality in a healthy, hierarchical organization. The model helps to identify many of the issues that have resulted in fuzzy hierarchy and unnecessary conflict over who owns what decision in an organization.

The key issue in board governance concerns the way in which the board of an organization relates to the staff of an organization. When this relationship is not clear, it has the potential to create a great deal of conflict, especially in terms of the ownership of decisions. This is certainly true in local congregations. Carver describes the increased attention that needs to be given concerning the decision making of nonprofit governing boards, "There has been a baffling failure to develop a coherent or universally applicable understanding of just what a board is for. While comparatively little thought has been given to developing governance theory and models, we have seen management of nonprofit organizations transform itself over and over again. Embarrassingly, however, boards do largely what they have always done."[9]

The conflicts that often arise between the governing board of a local congregation and the staff of the congregation generally are not the result of the individuals involved. However, this is often the case that is made. The assumption is that if everyone would simply function in a gracious, Christ-like manner, then any organizational structure can work. This argument has been used over and over again to minimize the importance of a healthy structure and organizational clarity.

The issue, however, is rarely limited to attitudes and personalities and instead involves the decision-making ethos itself. This is evidenced by the reoccurrence of conflicts in local congregations even though the individuals involved change over time. The similarity of these conflicts, which occur from generation to generation and across the entire church landscape, point to something more than simply individuals behaving badly. Carver argues that, typically, the issue is not the individuals involved but the structure itself. He says, "Boards tend to be, in fact, incompetent groups of competent individuals."[10]

The same could be said for many governing boards of local congregations. In most cases, the problem is not the competency or the commitment or the sincerity or the holiness of the board member. The problem is a system that fails to clarify what the board is responsible for and, even more importantly, what it is not responsible for. The demonizing of board members or the demonizing of the pastor accomplishes little. Organizations may change the players, and things might function with a little less conflict for a while, but eventually the same conflicts will arise. Sadly, many congregations never learn this lesson.

What is the primary responsibility of the governing board of a local congregation? Carver believes it has to do with making sure the organization accomplishes its stated purpose. He says, "Since the actual running of the organization is substantially in the hands of management, then it is important to the board that management be successful. The board must therefore increase the likelihood that management will be successful, while making it possible to recognize whether or not it really is successful."[11]

Many congregations struggle to define what missional success looks like. They may hesitate to define it out of a misguided fear that doing so will somehow make the activity of the church less spiritual. Without clarity, missional success becomes an ever-changing target. Staff members, particularly the senior pastor, are never quite sure whether the congregation is moving in the right direction.

Additionally, if the board is unclear about the definition of missional success, they never feel free to release the staff to make the necessary decisions to achieve it. This often results in the board's over-involvement in decision making. In this all too common scenario, the board may not know how success is going to be evaluated, but at least they have the comfort of knowing they were involved in making decisions in a vaguely defined effort to accomplish it. Carver explains, "The tradition-blessed habit of board approvals is a poor substitute for setting criteria, then checking that they have been met."[12] The result is staff members who feel restrained and unable to do what they believed they were placed in their position to do. He goes on to say, "Boards have had a very hard time knowing what to control and how to control it. The task is to demand organizational achievement in a way that empowers the staff, leaving to their creativity and innovation as much latitude as possible."[13]

Relationship Between the Senior Pastor and the Board

A key issue in most congregations is the relationship between the senior pastor and the board. A healthy decision-making ethos in a local congregation requires a clear and unique relationship between the senior pastor and the board. If there are several staff members who are directly accountable to the governing board, this inevitably results in confusion concerning who is responsible for what in the organization. Carver describes the way in which this unique relationship should function: "We recommend that the board use a single point of delegation and hold this position accountable for meeting all the board's expectations for organizational performance. The board, in effect, has one employee. Naturally, it is essential that the board delegate to this position all the authority that such extensive accountability deserves."[14] In the local congregation, this "single point of delegation" should be reserved for the senior pastor. Entrusting the senior pastor with both the authority and accountability for organizational performance simplifies the board's job and alleviates them of having to manage the internal, often complex, role responsibilities of the staff.

Hiring and Firing

Clarifying the board relationship to the senior pastor is crucial, particularly as a congregation and staff grow. If the board is directly involved in managing the work or evaluating the performance of staff who report to the senior pastor, it can result in a great deal of confusion and unnecessary conflict. This is especially true in the area of hiring and firing staff. In many congregations, this process is often very unclear. Sometimes the board, by being involved in the approval process, assumes the responsibility for hiring staff. However, in many cases, the board is not responsible for the firing of staff. This responsibility gap results in a certain degree of ambiguity concerning who is actually empowered to make the decision of letting a staff person go. In many instances, this ambiguity is exploited by departing staff members or congregational members who are sympathetic to staff members who are leaving.

Sometimes the entire congregation may be involved in approving the hiring of a particular staff member. Rarely, however, does the entire congregation participate in letting a staff member go. Again, this ambiguity is often exploited when the departure of a staff member is somewhat controversial or especially difficult. In some cases, the staff may be empowered to hire, but the firing of a staff member requires board approval. This results in a subtle undermining of the authority of staff members who have supervisory responsibility. Clarifying the relationship between the senior pastor and the board and making sure that the board is not directly involved in managing the work or evaluating the performance of staff, empowers the senior pastor to effectively lead the organization.

What Decisions Should the Board Make?

What decisions should be the responsibility of the governing board and what decisions should be the responsibility of the senior pastor and the staff? If these parameters are not established, a constant tension results over who is responsible for what decision. As mentioned earlier, much of the conflict in churches over decision making does not concern actual decisions but who was empowered to make them. This ambiguity can be addressed in the bylaws of the congregation. If it is clearly stated what decisions the board must make (and what decisions the congregation must make in churches with a more congregational form of government) then the myriad of other decisions can be entrusted to the senior pastor and those to whom he or she may delegate those decisions.

Invariably, specific decisions that have not been anticipated and that need to be guided by a broader decision-making principle will arise. Some organizations place those decisions in one of two categories—governance decisions and administrative decisions. That delineation, however, is not adequate for local congregations. The senior pastor of a local congregation is certainly more than an administrator of an organization. Administration describes only one aspect of a senior pastor's responsibility and certainly not its entirety. Decisions related to the vision and direction of the congregation, theological clarity, and the way in which the mission of the church is articulated also fall within the senior pastor's purview.

In a local congregation, innumerable decisions must be made on a daily basis. There must be some way of clarifying which decisions need to involve the board and which decisions are entrusted to the staff. Carver classifies these decisions into one of two categories. The first category includes those decisions that define organizational purpose, the *ends*. The second category includes all those decisions that do not define organizational purpose, the *means*.[15] Carver explains the difference between these two categories of decisions: "Ends never describe the organization itself or its activities. Ends are about the organization's impact on the world that justify its existence. Any decision that is not an ends decision is a means decision."[16] Most decisions made in a local congregation are means decisions, yet the fact that a particular decision is a means decision does not lessen its importance. Extremely important means decisions take place in local congregations. All decisions relating to personnel, financial planning and management, specific programs and ministries, teaching series and resources, and worship style are means decisions. To some degree, even decisions related to governance are means decisions. No church was ever started simply for the purpose of being well governed.

In local congregations that have a healthy decision-making ethos, the board will give the staff the maximum range in making means decisions. This is the reason staff members were hired. They possess the skills necessary to develop the means required to accomplish the stated purpose. The board may delineate specific means that it does not want the staff to use. These may be means that are contradictory to the purpose of the local congregation or are in conflict with biblical principles or ethical standards. This, however, would be a very finite list of means to avoid and would not require the board to be involved with the ongoing task of developing best practices.

Allowing the staff a great deal of freedom in making means decisions offers several advantages. It allows the organization to be much more agile in responding to ministry needs and opportunities. In addition, it avoids the awkward situation of board members supervising the work of highly trained, full-time professionals. Lastly, a decision-making ethos where all means decisions that are not prohibited are, in effect, pre-approved, relieves the board of the cumbersome and inefficient process of approving staff decisions.

The Problem with Committees

Another organizational practice, the formation of committees, contributes to a fuzzy hierarchy in many congregations. Some congregations have a myriad of committees that are, at best, vague in terms of responsibility and authority. In smaller churches these committees often are created to help the senior pastor accomplish the work of the congregation. As the congregation grows and additional staff members hired, the relationship between staff members and committees becomes unclear. Is the staff member responsible to the committee? Does the staff member have dual accountability to the committee and another staff member?

This hierarchical ambiguity often results in repetitious, parallel conversations with different groups in order to make one decision. A staff member first talks with the staff member to whom they are responsible, and perhaps with other congregational members, in an effort to make a good decision. Next the staff member takes what he or she considers the appropriate decision to the committee for its approval. But is it the committee's decision to approve? Who owns the decision? Does the committee own the decision or does the staff member own the decision? This is often unclear. Many congregations operate with the hope that everyone will agree on all aspects of the decision, and thereby the ownership question can be avoided altogether. In many situations, however, staff and committee do not achieve universal agreement, and unnecessary conflict results.

There is another way. Committees that are formed to assist the senior pastor or staff in the accomplishment of their responsibilities should be avoided. These types of committees include personnel committees, finance committees, Christian education committees, building and grounds committees, missions committees and youth ministry committees. All of these, and others like them, focus on means decisions. The rationale for these committees generally centers on the desire to mobilize the congregation for ministry. Much better ways exist, however, to mobilize the congregation. The staff operates with freedom to involve all the persons needed to carry out a particular ministry, and in fact, scripture enjoins them to do so. Paul calls pastors and teachers "to prepare God's people for works of service."[17] Staff can effectively mobilize the congregation without creating committees that create hierarchical confusion.

Hierarchical clarity hinges on who is mobilizing the congregation for ministry. When the board creates a committee to accomplish ministry, the relationship between the committee and staff is unclear. If a staff member mobilizes a group of people to accomplish ministry, hierarchical clarity is maintained. Boards may create committees, but they should be limited to committees that help the board to do its own job, not that of the staff.

Hierarchy in the New Testament

Chapter 6 takes a more expanded look at the focus of this book in light of the biblical narrative. At this point, however, it may be helpful to look briefly at five New Testament passages that seem to validate the role of hierarchy in the church. Hebrews 13 provides a strong endorsement of leadership in the local congregation. The notion that the first-century church was a community of Christ followers operating entirely on consensus without the presence of any hierarchical leadership does not seem to reflect the New Testament narrative. Not only was there identified leadership in the church, those leaders exerted a great deal of authority. The writer of Hebrews uses the word "obey" to describe the posture of the faith community to those who had been identified as leaders. The writer says, "Obey your leaders and submit to their authority. They keep watch over you as men who must give an account. Obey them so that their work will be a joy, not a burden, for that would be of no advantage to you."[18]

In the New Testament, the term "overseer" is an

1

important one. Jesus is described as the "Overseer of your souls." The text in 1 Peter 2 reads, "He himself bore our sins in his body on the tree, so that we might die to sins and live for righteousness; by his wounds you have been healed. For you were like sheep going astray, but now you have returned to the Shepherd and Overseer of your souls."[19] The fact that the term overseer is also used to describe the role of leaders in local congregations strongly endorses the empowering of visionary leadership in congregational life.

As Paul prepares to go to Jerusalem for what he knows will be a certain death sentence, he writes to the leaders in churches he helped to start. Paul refers to them as overseers and entrusts them with a protective role over their congregations. He says, "Keep watch over yourselves and all the flock of which the Holy Spirit has made you overseers. Be shepherds of the church of God, which he bought with his own blood."[20] The role of the congregational leader is unmistakable. Paul does not merely address a community. He addresses those within the community who have been given the mantle of leadership and the responsibility of protecting the church from "savage wolves" who desire to do harm to the church. In 1 Timothy 3, the qualifications for overseer are specifically articulated.

> Here is a trustworthy saying: If anyone sets his heart on being an overseer, he desires a noble task. Now the overseer must be above reproach, the husband of but one wife, temperate, self-controlled, respectable, hospitable, able to teach, not given to drunkenness, not violent but gentle, not

> quarrelsome, not a lover of money. He must
> manage his own family well and see that
> his children obey him with proper respect.
> (If anyone does not know how to manage
> his own family, how can he take care of
> God's church?) He must not be a recent
> convert, or he may become conceited
> and fall under the same judgment as the
> devil. He must also have a good reputa-
> tion with outsiders, so that he will not fall
> into disgrace and into the devil's trap.[21]

The specificity of these qualifications is intriguing. Clearly, the individuals Paul addresses are viewed not only as leaders by the congregation but also by the broader community. These individuals represent the church in a different way than other members of the congregation. Some type of hierarchical structure exists within the congregation, and these individuals have been entrusted with positional leadership and authority. For them to fail morally or to behave in an unethical way reflects on the entire church.

In 1 Peter 5, these overseers are referred to as elders. The admonition to the elders to not "lord" their leadership authority over other members of the congregation demonstrates the hierarchical nature of their role:

> To the elders among you, I appeal as a
> fellow elder, a witness of Christ's suffer-
> ings and one who also will share in
> the glory to be revealed: Be shepherds
> of God's flock that is under your care,

serving as overseers--not because you
must, but because you are willing, as
God wants you to be; not greedy for
money, but eager to serve; not lording
it over those entrusted to you, but being
examples to the flock. And when the Chief
Shepherd appears, you will receive the
crown of glory that will never fade away.[22]

Evidently these elders have been entrusted with a great
deal of positional authority within the congregation. So
much so, that the possible abuse of power is very real.
Therefore, the writer of Hebrews redefines the role of leadership to include radical servanthood. Christ becomes the
example of a true leader. Rather than dismantle the hierarchical structure, the attitude and focus of those entrusted
with positional authority is re-imagined.

Chapter Summary

The result of the surveys completed by the staffs of the
six congregations that are the focus of this book indicated
a high degree of hierarchical structure present in the
organization. The interviews with senior pastors of these
congregations reflected that as well. The need for clarity
in the hierarchy seemed to increase as the congregation
grew. In some cases, the congregation transitioned from
a fuzzy hierarchy to a better-defined hierarchy. Clarifying
the role of the board is essential in moving from a fuzzy
hierarchy to one that increases the possibility of missional
success. This clarification must address the relationship

of the senior pastor and the board, parameters of board decisions, and role of committees. There does seem to be the presence of some hierarchical structure in congregational life as described in the New Testament. Leaders are identified, given specific roles, held accountable, and warned to not abuse their positional leadership.

4 | The Case for Collaboration

ONE MIGHT ASSUME THAT SINCE ALL SIX CONGREGA-tions that were surveyed for this book scored high on hierarchy that they must have scored relatively low on collaboration. Even if the two were not pitted against one another, one might assume that highly hierarchical congregations would not be very collaborative in the way they make decisions. That assumption, however, would be wrong. Not only did all six of these congregations score high on hierarchy, they also scored high on collaboration. The possible results ranged from hardly any collaboration in making decisions (1) to extremely collaborative (5). As shown in the following graph, all but seven of the seventy-three staff members surveyed scored in the high collabora-tive quadrant (next page).

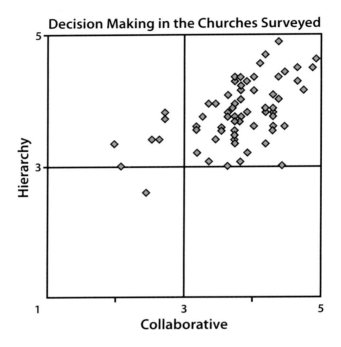

Illustration 2. Decision Making in Churches Surveyed

The Importance of Gathering

The senior pastors' narratives concerning the decision-making ethos of their congregations reinforce these
high collaborative scores. One reoccurring theme among
the senior pastors of these large, growing congregations
was the importance of regularly meeting as a staff. Steve
Treash, senior pastor at Black Rock Congregational
Church, talks about the need for intentionality in creating a
collaborative atmosphere among the staff, "I've chosen to

take a very collegial atmosphere in our staff. You can see it in the way we run our staff meetings and the way we do our staff agendas. We meet between three and four hours every Tuesday morning. We have an agenda that includes decisions that need to be made concerning church-wide strategy. The whole staff gets equal opportunity to feed into and discuss those issues. That's a very high value at the staff level."[1]

Harry Kuehl, senior pastor at The Church at Rancho Bernardo, constantly nurtures a culture of collaboration. One of the resources he has on staff for doing so is Lead Pastor Jeanette Moffett. Kuehl describes the specific gifts that Moffett possesses in this area and how she creates a culture of collaboration among the staff, "Jeanette is a real community person, so she's always putting together meetings in order to foster a sense of openness and trust. There's a real sense of love between staff. I think that's directly related to Jeanette bringing us together. We celebrate, appreciate, recognize milestones, and lift staff members up when there's a defining moment in their life."[2]

Not all people collaborate in the same way and recognizing the different collaborative styles of individuals is important. Individuals vary in the way they process information. Some tend to function best by processing individually and then sharing the results of their deliberation in a well thought out fashion to a wider audience. Others process better in groups. For some, the very process of the dialogue helps the individual decision-maker to think more clearly about the issue. Mark Batterson, senior pastor at

National Community Church tends to be the former. He says, "By default, I'm more of a personal processor."[3] Yet, in the context of his role as senior pastor, Batterson recognizes the importance of gathering in order to foster an atmosphere of collaboration. The way his creative team functions offers an example: "We have a creative team that consists of our worship pastor, media pastor and executive pastor. I meet with that team. We collaborate about messages, sermon branding, and order of service. The creative process is very collaborative."[4] A similar collaborative process occurs with other teams at National Community. However, the way in which each team collaborates may look very different depending on the nature of the team and the personalities involved. Understanding how people most effectively collaborate enables staff members to function at their highest level.

Leading from the Center

Much has been written on the value of collaboration in an organizational context. Often, however, these texts pit collaborative decision making against hierarchy and see the two as incompatible. In their book, *The Web of Women's Leadership: Recasting Congregational Ministry*, Susan Willhauck and Jacqulyn Thorpe use web terminology to make the case for the superiority of a collaborative decision-making ethos over one that is more hierarchical. They believe that the hierarchical model for leadership and decision- making is outdated, male oriented, and does not produce the greatest amount of health within organizations. According to Willhauck and Thorpe, the key difference between web-oriented leadership and traditional hierarchical leadership is the position from which the leader leads: "The most obvious architectural characteristic of the web is that it builds from the center out, and this building is a never-ending process."[5]

Willhauck and Thorpe believe that the positioning of the leader in the *center* of the organization as opposed to the *top* of the organization is an essential element of healthy organizations. They argue that leading from the top down tends to isolate leaders from those they are leading and emphasizes positional authority over relational authority. They believe that leaders who lead from the center are better positioned to be in relational connectedness with others in the organization: "One advantage of the web over the hierarchical system is that the leader in the center can connect all around instead of just downward."[6]

Avoiding Institutionalization

In his dissertation, *Organizational Structure, Religious Belief, and Resistance: The Emerging Church*, Josh Packard also makes the case for the abandonment of hierarchy in the decision-making structure of the church. Packard sees hierarchy as one of the forces that compel organizations toward institutionalization. He envisions the emerging church as a "resistant organization," which can resist institutionalization, in part, by pursuing a decision-making ethos that is not hierarchical. This abandonment of hierarchy is rooted in the belief that hierarchy creates a decision-making ethos that distances the decision makers from those who actually have the greatest expertise on a particular issue.

Packard argues that the emerging church can resist institutional pressures by creating a "fluid organizational structure" that adopts a shifting base of authority and context specific governance.[7] A shifting base of authority results in authority not being allocated on the basis of position but rather on expertise and desire. Context specific governance means that the decision-making structure changes, as do the people making the decisions, depending on the issue being addressed. The way in which a decision is made, therefore, is not determined a priori but rather on the spot. It is determined by the makeup of the participants and the specifics of the decision being made.[8]

A New Community

Gilbert Bilezikian advances a more collaborative view of the decision-making ethos of local congregations based on the kind of community seen in the New Testament church. The oneness of the Godhead shapes Bilezikian's view of community.

There are several implications of this particular view. Bilezikian's radical rejection of any type of hierarchical structure within the community of the church pertains directly to the focus of this book. He argues that since true community reflects the trinitarian nature of God and since there exists no ontological hierarchy between the Father, Son and Holy Spirit, then true community must be devoid of hierarchical structures of any kind except in the most dire of circumstances. He believes that in the new community of the church, no persons should be placed in subordination to other persons. He writes, "Before sin came into the world, there was no concern with structures of authority among humans and no need for such—only complete reciprocity."[9] Bilezikian sees hierarchy as the result of sin and judgment that has been nullified by the cross. He believes the New Testament gives witness to a new type of community—one of mutual submission (Ephesians 5:21) and very few structures—in the place of hierarchy.

Bilezikian argues that this new community operates solely on the basis of the gifts of the Spirit without regard to ethnicity, gender, status, or any other distinction that the sinful world may use to establish positions of authority and power. "Among mutually submitted and servant-minded individuals, gift-specific leadership is offered and accepted on the basis of competency rather than other considerations such as rank or gender."[10] Every instance in the New Testament where a particular individual or group within the church may seem to have been given a place of preeminence or in some cases a subordinate role, Bilezikian attributes to the unique and sometimes extraordinary circumstances surrounding the situation, and he warns against universalizing the particularities of those specific situations.

The Priesthood of All Believers

Greg Ogden advances a view of a more collaborative approach to decision making in the local church based on the priesthood of all believers. Ogden proposes that the Protestant Reformation gave the church a theological framework from which to embrace the priesthood of all believers, but that the church failed to fully seize this opportunity. He writes, "In spite of the Reformation, clericalism has more often than not held sway."[11]

Ogden quotes David Watson who observes, "Most Protestant denominations have been as priest-ridden as Roman Catholic. It is the minister, vicar, or pastor who has dominated the whole proceedings. In other words, the clergy-laity divisions have continued in much the same way as in pre-Reformation times, and the doctrine of spiritual gifts and body ministry have been largely ignored."[12] Ogden asserts that the reason that the Reformation was never able to realize the full potential of the priesthood of all believers was because it never really addressed or changed the institutional, hierarchical nature of the church. Unfortunately, he says, the Reformation "attempted to wed this organismic doctrine to an institutional definition of the church."[13]

A Starfish Rather
than a Spider

Ori Brafman and Rod A. Beckstrom make a compelling case for collaboration in their book, *The Starfish and the Spider: The Unstoppable Power of Leaderless Organizations*. The book focuses on the power of decentralized organizations, and views hierarchy as an obstacle to be overcome if organizations are going to reach their full potential. The title of the book reveals the metaphor that drives the argument. Brafman and Beckstrom begin with a detailed description of what distinguishes a spider from a starfish in terms of the interconnectedness of their various body parts: "Most of us know that a spider is a creature with eight legs coming out of a central body. With a magnifying glass, we can see that a spider also has a tiny head and eight eyes. If you chop off the spider's head, it dies. It could maybe survive without a leg or two, and could possibly even stand to lose a couple of eyes, but it certainly couldn't survive without its head."[14]

They go on to explain that while the starfish and the spider may look somewhat similar in their appearance, they are structured in fundamentally different ways:

> Like a spider, the starfish appears to have a bunch of legs coming out of a central body. But that's where the similarities end. The starfish doesn't have a head. Its central body isn't even in charge. In fact, the major organs are replicated throughout each and every arm. If you cut the starfish

in half, you'll be in for a surprise: the
animal won't die, and pretty soon you'll
have two starfish to deal with. They can
achieve this magical regeneration because
in reality, a starfish is a neural network—
basically a network of cells. Instead of
having a head, like a spider, the starfish
functions as a decentralized network. For
the starfish to move, one of the arms must
convince the other arms that it's a good
idea to do so. The arm starts moving, and
then in a process that no one fully understands the other arms cooperate and move
as well. The brain doesn't "yea" or "nay"
the decision. The starfish doesn't have
a brain. There is no central command.
Biologists are still scratching their
heads over how this creature operates.[15]

Brafman and Beckstrom argue that the most resilient
organizations are starfish-type organizations. They draw
their examples both from ancient cultures and twenty-first
century organizations.

The Aztecs and the Apache

The Aztecs, Brafman and Beckstrom write, were
organized like a spider. They had a clear and definable
head (Montezuma II) and a hierarchical organizational
structure. This, the authors contend, was the major contributing factor in the Aztecs destruction by Cortes and the

Spanish Army: "By 1521, just two years after Cortes first laid eyes on Tenochtitlan, the entire Aztec empire—a civilization that traced its roots to centuries before the time of Christ—had collapsed. The Aztecs weren't alone. A similar fate befell the Incas."[16]

When the Spanish Army encountered the Apache, however, the results were very different. The Spanish lost and Brafman and Beckstrom reason that the Apache were able to survive the hostile advances of the Spanish because the Apache were structured more like a starfish than a spider. They were decentralized with no singular, identifiable leader. This decentralized, non-hierarchical structure made them much more resilient to the advances of the Spanish Army. In examining the organizational structure of the Apache, Brafman and Beckstrom draw heavily from the research of Tom Nevins, a cultural anthropologist specializing in Native American tribes of the Southwest. Nevins identifies the organizational changes that took place among the Apache that lead to their eventual defeat. Interestingly enough, his work revolves around a change in their decision-making ethos.

The Apache were a threat until 1914. One of the main reasons they were so difficult to defeat was the way in which the Nant'ans functioned. The Nant'ans were basically men of wisdom that the Apache often looked to for guidance in making decisions. Their position had no real power associated with it. No one reported to the Nant'ans. Their authority was based primarily on their influence, and their influence was based on their actions and behaviors.

There were many Nant'ans among the Apache, so when
one was captured or isolated from the larger group another
Nant'an would quickly emerge. The Americans finally
"realized that they needed to attack the Apache at a very
basic level in order to control them. It was a policy they
first pioneered with the Navajo—who also were an Apache
group—and they perfected with the Western Apache
group."[17] What was their strategy? They gave the Nant'ans
cattle, and that changed everything. The Nant'ans then had
positional power based on the fact that they were in charge
of distributing this precious resource. Nevins points out,
"The power structure, once flat, became hierarchical, with
power concentrated at the top. With a more rigid power
structure, the Apaches became similar to the Aztecs, and
the Americans were able to control them."[18]

Alcoholics Anonymous

Brafman and Beckstrom make a similar case for a
non-hierarchical, decentralized, and purely collaborative
organization using Alcoholics Anonymous (AA) as an
example. They write, "At Alcoholics Anonymous, no one's
in charge. And yet, at the same time, everyone's in charge
. . . the organization functions just like a starfish. Thus, AA
is constantly changing form as new members come in and
others leave. The one thing that does remain constant is
the recovery principle—the famous twelve steps."[19] They
maintain that this non-hierarchical structure changes the
decision-making ethos of the organization: "Because there

is no one in charge, everyone is responsible for keeping themselves—and everyone else—on track. Even seniority doesn't matter that much . . . you have a sponsor, like a Nant'an, but the sponsor doesn't lead by coercion; that person leads by example."[20]

Brafman and Beckstrom contend this kind of non-hierarchical, decentralized structure creates a superior decision-making ethos because "each member has access to knowledge and the ability to make direct use of it."[21] In most organizations, knowledge and information are spread throughout the organization. In fact, some of the most helpful knowledge is often located at the fringe of the organization. A decentralized structure makes it easier to access that knowledge and use it to make good decisions.

Chapter Summary

The result of the surveys completed by the staffs of the six congregations that are the focus of this book indicated a high degree of collaboration present in the decision-making ethos of the organization. The fact that staff members also scored their organization high on hierarchical structure did not seem to negatively impact the degree of collaboration that took place in decision making. The interviews with the senior pastors of these congregations also reflected a high value on collaboration.

Much of what is written about the value of collaboration takes a negative view of hierarchical structure. Willhauck and Thorpe argue for the need for leaders to "lead from the center." They propose a structure that looks more like a web than a hierarchical organizational chart. Packard urges congregations to resist institutionalization and adopt a leadership structure with a shifting base of authority. Bilezikian envisions a new community devoid of any hierarchical structure functioning entirely on gift-based ministry. Ogden believes the priesthood of all believers should effectively dismantle the institutional nature of the church. Brafman and Beckstrom champion the value of a decentralized organization that more closely resembles a starfish rather than a spider. Each argument has merit, but as the next chapter will explore, is not necessarily incompatible with the presence of a clearly defined hierarchical structure.

5 | Charting a Third Way - Collaborative Hierarchy

WHICH DECISION-MAKING ETHOS—HIERARCHICAL or collaborative—is better suited to help growing congregations accomplish their mission and continue to grow? The answer is both. A non-hierarchical, completely decentralized, consensus-based decision-making ethos is not the goal. Those who try to make the case for such underestimate the value of hierarchy. A closer examination of the arguments made against hierarchy in the previous chapter reveals some flaws.

The Need for Leadership

Bilezikian's view of mutual submission is to be commended, especially as it relates to the role of women in the local congregation (a group that has often been excluded in the hierarchical structure of the church). His view of oneness rooted in the oneness of the trinitarian

God is both biblical and incredibly relevant to the issues facing the church today. However, the oneness of the trinitarian God need not automatically result in the demonizing of hierarchy. The presence of hierarchy in the New Testament narrative is hard to ignore. The fact that the apostle Paul lists leadership as one of the spiritual gifts seems to support at least some form of hierarchy, regardless of how flat one may contend that hierarchy is. The role of apostle itself seems to point toward hierarchy.

Bilezikian attempts to simultaneously redefine spiritual leadership in the church and do away with the need for it all together. He speaks of the need for spiritual leaders to have a servant mindset and to lead from a position of service rather from a position of power and authority. At the same time, he views authority within the church as a direct affront to the oneness that God desires for this new community. According to Bilezikian, authority should be exercised only in times of theological or moral crisis. He writes, "[The] appeal to authority for cases of exception indicates that relations of authority cannot be accepted as the modus operandi or as the normative way of doing church work under usual circumstances. Recourse to authority is reserved, according to the New Testament, for the intervention in sinful or deleterious situations that require corrective action."[1]

This is, however, a rather schizophrenic view of authority in which a leader only exercises authority when a crisis arises. At all other times, decisions require a consensus of the entire church body. Bilezikian correctly asserts that the

New Testament witness does not call leaders to lead on the basis of power and control but rather out of a spirit of servanthood and mutual submission. A heavy-handed imposition of a leader's will, or even of a leader's interpretation of God's will, is not the modus operandi of the church. However, the authority to make decisions not only in times of crisis but also within the normative context of the ongoing life of the community seems implicit in the role of congregational leadership. Decision making on the basis of reaching a consensus of the entire congregation does not seem to be wise or practical, nor does it appear to be mandated by the New Testament witness.

The situation that arose in Acts 6 where the Grecian widows were overlooked in the daily distribution of the food was met with a firm decision by the Twelve concerning how the matter would be handled. The situation the Twelve were dealing with could be described as neither "sinful" nor "deleterious" but simply reflective of the normal challenges of living in community. The community received their decision as authoritative and immediately implemented the plan. There is nothing inherent in hierarchy or in the authority given to church leaders that undermines the true community that God desires the church to experience. Rather, it is the sinful abuse of hierarchy and authority that destroys community.

Organizations and Organisms

Ogden deals with the decision-making ethos of a local congregation within the context of what he calls an "organismic" model of church structure. Like Bilezikian, he believes that all ministry within the church should take place on the basis of spiritual gifts. Positions and roles in the church should flow naturally from the specific spiritual gifts that a person possesses. Ogden concedes, however, that there is an organizational reality at work in the midst of this organismic model. He says, "This is not to say that the New Testament is uninterested in offices and structure. Rather, the key principle is that function precedes position. In other words, if authoritative leadership is translated into office, it is done only with the prior recognition that leadership has already been functioning."[2] This is a sound principle that, if regularly followed in congregational life, would lessen the chance that an individual not gifted for a significant role of leadership would be entrusted with that mantle.

Ogden is especially concerned about any title that would reinforce a hierarchical structure in the church, for example, senior pastor or associate pastor. However, he acknowledges the functional need for hierarchy when he says, "There must be a place where the buck stops and ultimate accountability resides. A ministry team can have shared responsibility, but there must be someone designated with the responsibility to enforce the accountability."[3] Ogden seems preoccupied with semantics at this point. There is a functional need for hierarchy in the life of the church. The local congregation is both an organism and an organization. A need exists for clear understanding of who is empowered with leadership and how each person in ministry relates to those leaders. The problem is not hierarchy per se but ill-equipped leaders within the hierarchy who fail to understand servant leadership.

Ogden hints at the idea of collaborative hierarchy when he notes the following characteristics of servant leaders.

- People in the highest positions of authority have the greatest obligation to serve.

- Servant leadership is rooted in relationship, not coercion.

- Servant leadership naturally seeks to support, not to control.

- Servant leaders shine the spotlight of recognition on those with whom they share leadership.[4]

When the lives of congregational leaders who function in a hierarchical structure manifest these characteristics, people will be valued, ministry will be released, and the organization will manifest a healthier decision-making ethos.

The Unnecessary
Dismantling of Hierarchy

Willhauck, Thorpe, and Packard highlight the importance of collaboration when they warn against a decision-making ethos where isolated leaders make unilateral
decisions based solely on their position in the organization. However, they assume this type of unhealthy decision
making can be addressed only by dismantling the hierarchical structure. Hierarchy does not negate collaborative
decision making in which leaders utilize the wisdom and
insights of a broad group of people in making a decision.
Hierarchy does not prevent leaders from being in significant relationships with a wide range of persons within the
organization. Clear lines of authority do not limit dialogue
throughout the organization.

Willhauck and Thorpe suggest that the organizational
chart of an organization must change if a healthy decision-
making ethos is to be established. A re-drawing of the
organization chart, however, is unnecessary and, in fact,
minimizes the primary issue they are trying to address.
Leading from the center reflects less about organizational
structure and more about organizational style. It is about
leading out of relational authority rather than positional
authority. Leading out of relational authority encourages
collaborative decision making. The leader's authority and
power comes from being accessible and dialogical rather
than merely from position. This, in turn, creates an environment in which more people participate in the decision-

making process and fewer people feel marginalized.

Packard ignores the benefit of hierarchy that allows churches to grow without creating organizational barriers to growth or requiring the church to fundamentally change its decision-making ethos. All of the emerging churches that Packard cites in his research are relatively small congregations. The larger an organization gets, the more important clarifying who is empowered to make particular decisions becomes.

Pushing the Starfish Metaphor

The further Brafman and Beckstrom push their starfish and spider metaphor, the clearer it becomes that most organizations cannot function purely as starfish. A deeper look at the story of the Apache and the non-hierarchical, decentralized decision-making ethos that allowed them to avoid defeat for so long reveals that pure decentralization is most effective when the primary goal is simply to survive. These movements are structured to disrupt more than they are structured to produce. In fact, once they begin to produce, the need for hierarchy begins to emerge. When the community needs decisions made concerning the distribution of resources or the accomplishment of a common mission, the non-hierarchical, decentralized structure no longer seems adequate.

Brafman and Beckstrom point out the shift that eventually took place in the decision-making ethos of Alcoholics Anonymous.

As an ultimate act of letting go, Bill W. and his fellow authors agreed that all proceeds from the work, nicknamed *The Big Book*, would go to support Alcoholics Anonymous World Services, Inc., a nonprofit dedicated to supporting chapters worldwide. These proceeds weren't very significant when Bill W. put together *The Big Book*; AA had only about a hundred members at the time. But AA eventually grew into more than 100,000 chapters. Copies of *The Big Book* sold like hotcakes over the years—22 million at last count. These unexpected book sales produced enormous revenues, all of which went to Alcoholics Anonymous World Services, Inc. What cows were to the Apache, book sales became to AA. As *Big Book* profits rolled in, the little nonprofit that they were supposed to fund ballooned into a huge, wealthy organization. When individual members of AA started translating *The Big Book* into various languages and giving it away for free, headquarters cracked down, even going so far as to sue members.[5]

The resources with which World Services was entrusted began slowly moving Alcoholics Anonymous toward centralization. The same principle applies to the providing of salaries to those who work for an organization. Organizations whose members work primarily as volunteers can be very non-hierarchical and decentralized. However, the introduction of salaries into the equation increases the need for hierarchy and control. The very nature of salaries necessitates an ethos in which decisions are made concerning salary amount and, in volunteer organizations like the local congregation, who gets a salary and who does not. Salaries, in turn, introduce the need to make decisions concerning hiring and firing and the clarifying of who is responsible for such decisions.

Wikipedia, the online encyclopedia maintained mostly by volunteers, presently faces an interesting dilemma: It makes too much money. This abundance of resources may lead to more salaried positions. If a large number of people start being paid, the volunteer dynamic that has driven the success of the organization will change and impact the decision-making ethos of the organization. Decisions, which previously were made in a decentralized, strictly collaborative manner and were enforced by the community, will need to be made within the context of increased centralization and hierarchy.

Is the Local Congregation a Starfish or a Spider?

What is the local congregation? Is it a starfish? Is it primarily a disruptive movement focused on what needs to be dismantled and destroyed within a culture that reflects so little of the kingdom? Or is it a spider? Is it an organization focused on advancing a shared identity and orthodoxy, and committed to the accomplishment of a common mission? It is both—hierarchical and collaborative. Brafman and

Beckstrom identify the balance between hierarchy and collaboration as the "sweet spot." They contend that every organization must find its sweet spot to be successful and that movement too far in either direction causes the organization to lose its edge. In his book, *Mosaic*, Patrick Nachtigall writes about the importance of hierarchy even in the midst of a growing movement toward collaboration and decentralization. "Hierarchical organizations also have the potential to create safeguards for the unity of the church by having clear lines of authority, channels of communication on important matters, and structures that clearly reveal who is accountable to whom."[6]

How does a local congregation develop a decision-making ethos that maintains the clarity and control that hierarchy provides and still maintains the dynamism and collective creativity and wisdom of collaboration? How does a congregation create an incubator for creative, innovative ideas and yet maintain a sense of common mission and focused direction? Collaborative hierarchy offers an answer to this dilemma.

Who Owns the Decision? Collaboration v. Consensus

One of the most important issues in the decision-making ethos of an organization is the question of who owns a particular decision. The issue of ownership focuses on which individual or group has been entrusted with the responsibility and the authority to make the decision. Many congregations rarely address decision ownership, and when they do their explanation of ownership reflects a vague recitation of the groups or individuals who may have some vested interest in the decision and therefore should have some say in making the decision. Oftentimes, however, congregations simply avoid the question of who really owns the decision and hope that all parties will find agreement with whatever decision has been made. In fact, failure to clarify the ownership of a decision may be seen as a positive. In the event that the decision is not warmly received, it then becomes easier for groups or individuals to distance themselves from the decision or place the blame on someone else.

In his book, *Scripture and Discernment—Decision Making in the Church*, Luke Timothy Johnson argues that in the local congregation, groups, rather than individuals, should make decisions. However, like so many, he makes no distinction between group decisions and individual decisions that are highly collaborative in their process. The failure to make this distinction often contributes to an unhealthy decision-making ethos.

Decisions that are owned by a group are typically characterized by consensus building. The goal of the leader, if a leader is identified, is to carefully and skillfully move the group toward consensus. In consensus decision making, the leader may assume one of two roles. He or she may lead as a primary influencer. In this role, the leader assumes that he or she already knows what decision needs to be made and must now help the group come to consensus around that decision.

Pastors often find themselves encouraged to assume the role of primary influencer. Many conferences and seminars on church leadership begin with the assumption that pastors are in the best position to know what decisions need to be made in the life of the congregation. Because of the decision-making ethos of the church, however, they may not have permission to make those decisions. Therefore, the role of the pastor is to gently build consensus among the decision-making group around the decision the pastor already feels compelled to make. This influencing role can occur in the context of the meeting itself as the pastor winsomely makes his or her case for a particular decision or it can take place outside of the meeting by talking with each member of the group individually. The goal is the same. The pastor attempts to build consensus for a decision he or she has already become convinced is the right decision. In light of the decision-making ethos of the congregation, this approach may be viewed as being politically expedient but it seems inauthentic at best and manipulative at worst.

The other role the leader can assume in decision making by consensus is the role of unbiased facilitator, in which the leader focuses simply on facilitating the process by which the group arrives at a decision. As the facilitator, the leader does not maintain a strong position concerning the impending decision, and when the process is facilitated well, a decision emerges from the group. There are, of course, a number of other variations on these two roles and on decision making by consensus.

In collaborative hierarchy, the individual typically owns the decision. The individual may seek counsel from any number of individuals or groups, but the decision clearly belongs to the individual. When an organization seeks to be collaborative without the presence of clear hierarchy, unnecessary conflicts arise. In addition, when leaders function within a decision-making ethos that fails to empower the leader with the necessary authority to make the required decisions to effectively lead the organization, diversionary techniques are often utilized.

One such diversionary technique is appropriately named the "garbage-can theory." The garbage-can theory arises from the concept that most group decisions do not actually solve problems but instead defer them to another day. Rather than identifying a problem, generating alternative solutions, gathering as much information as possible, and then making a clear decision that solves the problem; most group-based decision-making processes are far more random. For instance, decisions may change depending upon who happens to be present at a particular meeting. Over time, even the definition of the available solutions from which to choose may change. In an often cited 1974 study of college presidents, James March and Michael Cohen found that presidents who wanted to get things done would often create arenas of discussion like strategic planning processes, retreats, and goal definition processes. These garbage-can activities would draw energy away from more important decisions, which the president could then control.[7]

Local congregations often employ the garbage-can model. The perceived need to include people in the decision-making process results in time-consuming and unproductive meetings where decisions are deferred to another day. When decisions are made, they are often unclear, poorly defined and open to different interpretations. The implied decision makers are groups of people who may vary in composition from meeting to meeting. In this decision-making ethos, leaders can spend an inordinate amount of time and energy either creating garbage-can arenas that provide the perception of participation or lobbying group members outside of the meetings in order to achieve the desired decision.

Conversely, a leader empowered as decision maker moves board conversations from diversion and persuasion to conversations seeking wise counsel. The senior pastor is not required to build consensus before making a decision but is free to pursue as much collaborative input as needed in order to make a good decision. This fundamentally changes the way the senior pastor relates to the board.

The pastors who were interviewed for this book expressed similar thoughts concerning the ownership of decisions by individuals rather than groups. Bishop Thompson of Jubilee Christian Church said, "The elders sit over different areas in the church. Each elder is empowered to make certain decisions. However, their decisions are not decisions that they make in a vacuum."[8] Thompson's reference to decisions not being made in a vacuum acknowledges the role collaboration plays in the decisions of the individual elders. Each elder maintains close relationships with others who serve in their area of ministry. Conversations with their ministry team, as well as conversations with other elders and the senior pastor, inform the elders' decisions.

When Mark Batterson of National Community Church was asked about the ownership of decisions, he responded, "I think it's always an individual. I don't want to lead a team meeting without a clear understanding of who is responsible for what."[9] Marty Grubbs of Crossings Community Church responded to the same question by saying, "The individual ministry leader is the moral owner of the decision. However, they often arrive at a decision with the collaboration of a team."[10] In each case, value seems to be placed on individual ownership of decisions while at the same time promoting a culture where those decisions are not made in isolation.

Who is at the Table?

One of the prerogatives of leadership is the freedom to determine who to bring into the discussion when a decision is being made. In this context, hierarchical structure, departmental responsibility, and job description should be set aside for the purpose of making good decisions. The persons best positioned to contribute to a decision may even work outside the department that the decision most greatly impacts. They may be positioned several levels up or down the organizational chart from the person actually entrusted with the decision. They may be a member of the congregation with no official leadership role. However, they bring a skill set or perspective essential to the decision.

Many pastors fail in this aspect of developing a healthy decision-making ethos in the local congregation. They either fail to establish clear boundaries concerning areas of responsibility, or they become so rigid in those determinations that valuable insights for making good decisions never enter into the discussion. Those valuable insights are "locked away" two or three levels down in the organization, in another department, or within the membership of the congregation. This is a loss both for the pastor and for the congregation, and results in decision making that is uninformed, unchallenged, or premature.

Effective leaders operating in collaborative hierarchies surround themselves with others in the organization that have expertise, perspective, and experience that the leader does not possess. These are not always the same people, and which people are brought in to participate in a decision will depend on the particular issue being addressed. An organization that is strictly hierarchical may surround the leader with a small group of advisors who contribute to the decision-making process. This group, however, usually reflects position rather than giftedness or expertise. As a result the core group can insulate the leader, essentially isolating the leader from others in the organization.

In an organization that reflects a collaborative hierarchy, participatory decision making functions in a very different way. Trusted members of the organization who bring the most expertise and giftedness to the issue are sought out for the purpose of informing decisions. Different issues require that different groups of people be brought into the dialogue. Effective leaders will engage in a variety of conversations with diverse people in the organization in order to make wise, well-informed decisions. This process makes the isolation of the leader virtually impossible.

In terms of Willhauck's web metaphor, this decision-making process makes it possible for anyone in the organization to be brought to the center if they possess the necessary gifts, talents and passions on a particular issue, and are trusted by the leader. This process also allows leaders to get helpful feedback from others in the organization that they might not get because of where these persons are positioned in the organization. As an organization grows to several thousand, it becomes impossible to be in relationship with everyone in the organization. Even in large, hierarchical organizations, however, leaders can create an environment of collaboration rather than isolation.

Boundaryless Organizations

In the book, *The Boundaryless Organization*, Ron Ashkenas makes the case for hierarchies that have vertical and horizontal fluidity. In these boundaryless organizations, "behavior patterns conditioned by boundaries between levels, functions, and other constructs are replaced by patterns of free movement across these same boundaries." In this case, boundaries continue to serve a positive organizational purpose without ghettoizing resources and information. "Rather than using boundaries to separate people, tasks, processes, and places, organizations are beginning to focus on how to get through those boundaries—to move ideas, information, decisions, talent, rewards, and actions where they are most needed."[11]

This fluidity accurately reflects the culture present in a collaborative hierarchy. Ashkenas identifies four types of boundaries that characterize most organizations. The two that most often create organizational isolation in local congregations are, "vertical boundaries between levels and ranks of people, (and) horizontal boundaries between function and disciplines."[12] It is not that the boundaries are unimportant. They are, in fact, very important. As Ashkenas points out, "Boundaries keep things focused and distinct. Without them, organizations would be disorganized. People would not know what to do. There would be no differentiation of tasks, no coordination of resources and skills, no sense of direction. In essence, the organization would cease to exist."[13] A collaborative hierarchy does not require a removal of organizational boundaries. It simply requires that these boundaries be fluid rather than rigid.

Hierarchical structure and departments must allow for a fluidity of dialogue throughout the organization. Ashkenas utilizes a biological view of boundaries in describing this fluidity within the organization:

> In living organisms, membranes exist to provide shape and definition. They have sufficient structural strength to prevent its collapse into an amorphous mass. Yet, they are permeable. Food, oxygen, and chemical transmitters flow through them relatively unimpeded so that each part of the organism can contribute to the rest. So it is with a boundaryless organization. Information, resources, ideas, and energy pass through its membranes quickly and easily so that the organization as a whole functions effectively. Yet, definition and distinction still exist – there are still leaders with authority and accountability, (and) there are still people with special functional skills.[14]

In a collaborative hierarchy, which manifests much of the same organizational fluidity, communication becomes essential, and the communication must flow in all directions. Communication must flow vertically, up and down the hierarchy, and it must flow horizontally, across departmental boundaries. It is virtually impossible to over-communicate in an organization that desires a decision-making ethos that reflects collaborative hierarchy.

The Family as
a Metaphor for
Collaborative Hierarchy

In the Bible, the people of God are often referred to
in familial terms. They are called children of God, the
family of God, members of God's family, the household
of faith, brothers and sisters, heirs of God, and co-heirs
with Christ. Over the years, the church has used familial
language to describe itself. In my denomination, Church of
God (Anderson, IN), familial language was very common
in the early years of its existence. Men and women in
the church were often referred to as brothers and sisters.
Familial language even became a part of the songs that
were sung. The chorus and first verse to Bill Gaither's
song, *The Family of God*, says:

> I'm so glad I'm a part of the Family of
> God, I've been washed in the fountain,
> cleansed by His Blood! Joint heirs with
> Jesus as we travel this sod, for I'm part
> of the family, the Family of God. You will
> notice we say "brother and sister" 'round
> here, It's because we're a family and these
> are so near; When one has a heartache,
> we all share the tears, And rejoice in
> each victory in this family so dear.[15]

In spite of the frequent use of familial language,
however, the decision-making ethos of the local congregation has failed, at times, to reflect the insights that

the family model offers. The healthy family provides a helpful metaphor for thinking about the decision-making ethos of a local congregation. The nuclear family, where young children are at home and parents are present and engaged, displays a highly participatory decision-making process. Like most organizations, families have common goals they want to accomplish, important decisions they need to make, generational and personality differences that have to be dealt with, and a healthy culture that has to be maintained. Also, like most organizations, families have a degree of hierarchy in which certain individuals (parents) are entrusted with leadership responsibilities. While the hierarchy of the family is certainly very flat, it still requires parents to develop appropriate ways to communicate, evaluate, encourage, empower, and affirm other members of the family.

Collaborative hierarchy reflects a decision-making ethos that is familial in nature because of the high value it places on relationships. There is a high level of relational connectedness throughout the organization. Most decisions are made within the context of open and honest dialogue. Persons are included in the dialogue based on their gifts, talents and passions, not simply because of the position that they hold within the organization. While parents certainly have positional leadership within the family, healthy families require strong, growing relationships between members of the family. Organizations that maintain a collaborative hierarchy understand the importance of relationships and give time and energy to nurture those relationships. They understand the connection between healthy relationships within the organization and a healthy decision-making ethos.

In his book, *Leading Without Power*, Max DePree uses the family as a metaphor for healthy organizations. He says, "When we stop and think about it, a healthy family is perhaps the best example of a non-profit group!"[16] He identifies several characteristics of family life as necessary components in organizations. They include the demonstration of unconditional love; teaching and demonstrating a clear, concrete set of values; teaching appropriate social and functional skills; teaching how to manage resources; making learning a permanent part of life; exploring the future together; and celebrating together.[17] Each of these characteristics requires the establishing and maintaining of healthy relationships within the organization. They require the leader to engage in meaningful ways with others in the organization. The family model prevents leaders from becoming relationally disconnected from those who are further down the organizational chart. DePree says, "The longer I live and the more I see of organizations, the more I'm forced to the conclusion that at the heart of organizations is always this matter of competence in relationships."[18]

Families and Relational Accessibility

One distinctive characteristic of collaborative hierarchy is the relational accessibility of the leader of the organization. Clear lines of authority exist, yet the leader is not isolated relationally. In healthy families, the ones entrusted with decision-making authority (parents) are not isolated from the rest of the family. Relational connectedness takes place in a variety of ways. At times, the entire family may do something together, and at other times, Mom/Dad may spend time together by themselves. On one particular day, Dad may spend some special time with one child, and on another day, he may spend time with a different child. Mom may follow a similar pattern. A family includes many different relationship combinations, and healthy families seek to nurture all of them. This relationship matrix places the parents more in the center of the family rather than at the top of the family. The matrix does not change their leadership role or responsibility; it merely changes the way in which they lead. Their ability to lead is not based primarily on their position in the family but rather on their relational influence within the family.

This model holds true in organizations where collaborative hierarchy defines the decision-making ethos. The leader of the organization functions less from the top of the organization and more from the center. Again, clear lines of authority continue to exist, and everyone in the organization knows who has the authority to make certain decisions. Decision making, however, takes place within the context of a rich matrix of relationships and is generally highly participatory.

This does not mean that organizations can ignore the importance of hierarchy and positional authority. Again, the family provides a helpful metaphor. A healthy family does not ignore the positional authority of the parents. Situations arise when decisions need to be made on the basis of positional authority. The same pattern holds true in organizations that reflect a family model. However, leaders who lead from the center deemphasize positional authority. By positioning themselves to be in relational connectedness with others in the organization, the leaders create environments in which a greater number of people are included in the decision-making process, and fewer people feel marginalized based on their position within the hierarchy.

Collaborative Hierarchy in the Congregations Surveyed

All the congregations surveyed for this book identified a decision-making ethos that reflected collaborative hierarchy. As shown in the graph below, all but seven of the staff members surveyed fell into the high hierarchy/ high collaborative quadrant. (next page)

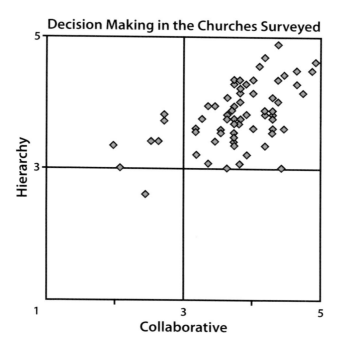

Illustration 2. Decision Making in Churches Surveyed

Responses by Gender

What is particularly interesting is that the answers given on the survey did not seem to be significantly impacted by gender or age. As can be seen from the chart below, the distribution pattern of answers within the high hierarchy/ high collaborative quadrant was similar between male and female respondents. Male respondents scored 3.86 on hierarchy and 3.75 on collaborative. Female respondents scored 3.82 on hierarchy and 3.68 on collaborative. (Appendix 3)

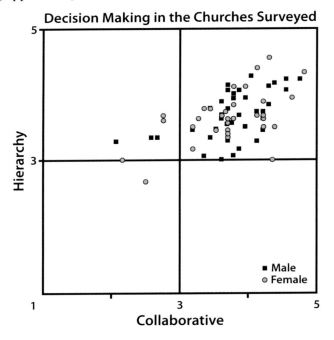

Illustration 3. Decision Making in Churches
Surveyed – Responses by Gender

Responses by Age

The same was true for age. Respondents were divided into four different age categories: 20-29, 30-39, 40-49, 50 and older. Again, the distribution pattern of answers within the high hierarchy/high collaborative quadrant was similar between each of the four age demographics.

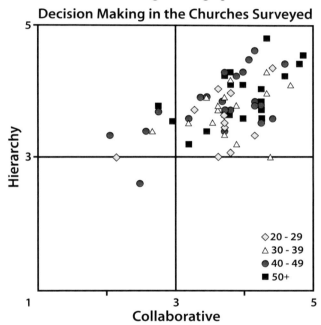

Illustration 4. Decision Making in Churches Surveyed –
Responses by Age.

The following graphs provide a separate view of each age demographic.

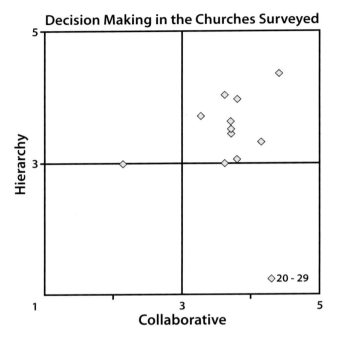

Illustration 5. Responses by Age 20-29

Illustration 6. Responses by Age 30-39

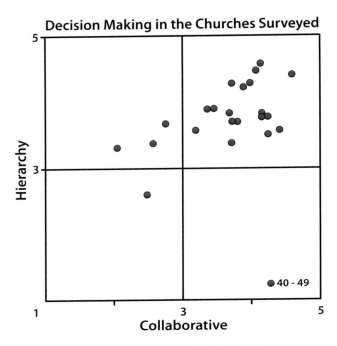

Illustration 7 Responses by Age 40-49

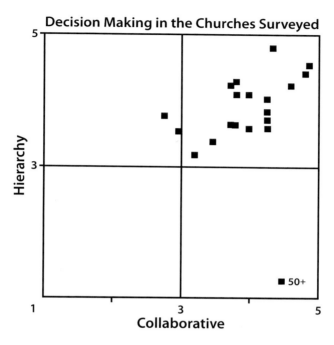

Illustration 8. Responses by Age 50+

While strikingly similar in distribution pattern, the age demographics reflect some subtle differences. Respondents in their twenties, on average, did not score as high in hierarchy (3.61) as respondents in their fifties (4.05). (Appendix 4) This may reflect some generational differences in how hierarchy is viewed among younger staff members.

In terms of collaboration, all of the age demographics are also very similar. The one interesting observation is that respondents in their fifties, on average, appear to view their decision-making ethos as slightly more collaborative than respondents in the three younger age categories. (Appendix 4) This subtle difference may reflect a tendency for staff members to value collaboration even more highly as they move into a season of ministry that is often characterized by more mentoring and an increased focus on the next generation. Again, these differences are subtle and should be viewed against the backdrop of a decision-making ethos in each of the congregations surveyed that overwhelming reflects collaborative hierarchy regardless of gender or age.

Chapter Summary

Local congregations can be both hierarchical and collaborative. It is not necessary to dismantle the hierarchical structure in order to achieve a collaborative environment. Leading from the center is less about organizational structure and more about organizational style. It does not do away with positional authority but re-envisions leadership based on relational influence. The family provides a useful metaphor for emphasizing the importance of this relational connectedness and accessibility.

In a collaborative hierarchy, individuals rather than groups generally own decisions. These individuals, however, tend to function in a highly collaborative way in making decisions, bringing whoever is needed into the conversation in order to make a good decision. Organizations with a decision-making ethos that reflects collaborative hierarchy possess a kind of fluidity in the organization, which allows information to move vertically between levels in the hierarchy and horizontally across departmental boundaries. The staffs of the six congregations surveyed for this book indicated the presence of both a high degree of hierarchy and collaboration in the decision-making ethos of these organizations. The survey results were not significantly impacted by age or gender.

6 | Collaborative Hierarchy and the Biblical Narrative

D IFFICULTY ARISES IN MAKING A BIBLICAL CASE FOR any particular form of church polity or decision-making structure. The New Testament does not clearly articulate structure concerning the local congregation, and the structure it does articulate seems to come to the surface only in relation to specific congregational issues that needed to be addressed. The lack of a definitive biblical structure for the local congregation is, no doubt, the primary reason for so many different decision-making structures within local congregations. There does, however, seem to be a decision-making ethos that emerges from the plurality of structures observed in scripture. This ethos is, at the very least, consistent with the idea of collaborative hierarchy.

Scripture focuses primarily, as it pertains to the role counsel plays in decision making, on the counsel of God. Leaders and kings are admonished to seek God's counsel. The counsel of God is set in contrast to the counsel of the wicked. This does not mean, however, that scripture speaks nothing about leadership and the role human counsel plays in decision making. One can construct a view of leadership that promotes isolation and minimizes the input of others. To do so, however, ignores the human agency that God utilizes to help leaders make good decisions. The writer of Proverbs says, "Plans fail for lack of counsel, but with many advisers they succeed."[1] The Bible repeatedly reinforces this admonition in Israel's narrative. When the leaders and kings of Israel, who were clearly entrusted with decision-making responsibility, rejected the wise counsel of others and made isolated decisions, their decisions often resulted in personal and national disaster.

The Acts 15 Decision

Acts 15 provides an excellent New Testament example of collaborative hierarchy. The question concerns what requirements should be placed on Gentiles who respond positively to the gospel of Jesus Christ. Verse 1 reads, "Some men came down from Judea to Antioch and were teaching the brothers: 'Unless you are circumcised, according to the custom taught by Moses, you cannot be saved.'"[2] The requirement of circumcision for Gentile converts created a great deal of distress and ultimately resulted in a meeting in Jerusalem of various leaders in the church. At the meeting, a number of persons expressed their views concerning how they believed the church should deal with this issue.

First, the account reads, "Then some of the believers

who belonged to the party of the Pharisees stood up and said, 'The Gentiles must be circumcised and required to obey the law of Moses.'"[3] Then Peter addressed the group:

> Brothers, you know that some time ago God made a choice among you that the Gentiles might hear from my lips the message of the gospel and believe. God, who knows the heart, showed that he accepted them by giving the Holy Spirit to them, just as he did to us. He made no distinction between us and them, for he purified their hearts by faith. Now then, why do you try to test God by putting on the necks of the disciples a yoke that neither we nor our fathers have been able to bear? No! We believe it is through the grace of our Lord Jesus that we are saved, just as they are.[4]

Barnabas and Paul add their counsel: "The whole assembly became silent as they listened to Barnabas and Paul telling about the miraculous signs and wonders God had done among the Gentiles through them."[5]

It is James, however, in the midst of this plurality of voices, who appears to be entrusted with making this decision. After listening to each person speak, James indicates his agreement with Peter and quotes the prophets concerning the role of the Gentiles in God's salvific plan. James then makes this definitive statement. "It is my judgment, therefore, that we should not make it difficult for the Gentiles who are turning to God. Instead we should write to them, telling them to abstain from food polluted by idols, from sexual immorality, from the meat of strangled animals, and from blood."[6] James's declaration that "it is my judgment" gives strong indication that he has been entrusted with the authority to make this particular decision.

The remaining narrative indicates that the other leaders who are present at the meeting embrace James's decision. In the letter they write to the Gentile believers in Antioch, Syria, and Cilicia communicating the decision they say, "It seemed good to the Holy Spirit and to us not to burden you with anything beyond the following requirements: You are to abstain from food sacrificed to idols, from blood, from the meat of strangled animals, and from sexual immorality."[7] At first glance, the phrase "It seemed good to the Holy Spirit and to us" seems to reflect consensus decision making. The context, however, indicates more of a collaborative hierarchy at work than decision by consensus. The church leaders who travelled to Jerusalem representing the party of the Pharisees were definitely on the other side of this issue. Scripture does not indicate that James brought the entire group of church leaders gathered in Jerusalem to a consensus prior to making his decision. Had James attempted to reach a consensus among all the church leaders, it could have resulted in a very different decision or perhaps even the postponement of a decision. The latter is often the result of consensus-based decision making, especially when the decision is a difficult one.

In this case, it appears that James listened to the input of the gathered group of leaders and then made what he believed was the right decision. Other church leaders then enthusiastically embraced his decision. Scripture does not say if all the church leaders embraced his decision, but in some ways it does not matter. A clear decision was made and broadly supported. Not only did other leaders in the church embrace it, the broader church community embraced it. When they delivered the letter to the believers in Antioch, the group enthusiastically received the decision: "So they were sent off and went down to Antioch. When they gathered the congregation together, they delivered the letter. When its members read it, they rejoiced at the exhortation."[8]

This passage offers a beautiful example of collaborative hierarchy within a church context. A church leader is clearly entrusted with a decision. He or she does not, however, make the decision in isolation. In making the decision, James chose not only to seek the input of numerous people but also to draw on the narrative of scripture and the narrative of experience.

In his book, *Scripture and Discernment—Decision Making In The Church*, Luke Timothy Johnson identifies three influences on decision making in the life of the church. They are the narrative of scripture, the narrative of community experience, and prayer.[9] The author argues that the narrative of experience is the lens through which the narrative of scripture is interpreted. James demonstrated this principle in his decision making in Acts 15. James viewed the words of the prophet concerning the role of the Gentiles in God's salvific plan through the narrative of experience to which Barnabas and Paul bore witness. The narrative of experience included the miraculous signs and wonders God had done among the Gentiles. James' reliance upon the narrative of scripture and the narrative of experience within the context of a collaborative process resulted not only in a good decision, but one embraced by others who were included in the dialogue.

Paul's Perspective of the Acts 15 Decision

In Galatians, Paul relates his perspective of the events of the council that took place in Jerusalem. He says, "I went in response to a revelation and set before them the gospel that I preach among the Gentiles. But I did this privately to those who seemed to be leaders, for fear that I was running or had run my race in vain."[10] Even though Paul experienced great success in his ministry, he still felt a sense of accountability to the leaders of the church. He refused to operate as a lone ranger in regard to this calling to take the gospel to the Gentiles. When Paul arrived in Jerusalem, he was warmly welcomed and given the opportunity to share what God was doing among the Gentiles. Paul describes that encounter: "James, Peter and John, those reputed to be pillars, gave me and Barnabas the right hand of fellowship when they recognized the grace given to me. They agreed that we should go to the Gentiles, and they to the Jews. All they asked was that we should continue to remember the poor, the very thing I was eager to do."[11] While Paul does not use decision-making language to describe this encounter, clearly he was presenting his case to those who had been entrusted with decision-making authority. The phrase, "they agreed" is Paul's way of talking about the decision made by James and enthusiastically embraced by Peter and John.

The decision-making process seen in Acts 15 stands in stark contrast to that which is often seen in local congregations. Many congregations spend a great deal of organizational energy clarifying who owns a particular decision. This lack of clarity frequently results in postponing decisions or in unnecessary conflict after decisions have been made. The conflict over who has the authority to make a particular decision often takes the focus away from the quality of the decision itself. The narrative of scripture and the narrative of experience become less important than making sure that everyone feels ownership for the decision. The result is endless discussion that circles around the same issues over and over again, and a misplaced hope that out of the discussion a clear and compelling decision will simply emerge. However, decisions rarely just emerge. Decisions must be made. When those decisions are consistent with the narrative of scripture, the narrative of experience, and are made within the context of a collaborative process, the leadership of the congregation and the congregation as a whole are very likely to enthusiastically embrace the decision that has been made.

Old Testament Examples of Collaborative Hierarchy

What about collaborative hierarchy in the Old Testament? Does scripture reveal collaborative hierarchy at work in the midst of this environment of strong leaders who God has raised up to lead a nation or is the decision-making ethos autocratic in its purest form? A brief review of several Old Testament passages reveals a surprising answer.

Moses and Jethro

The story of Moses and his father-in-law, Jethro, offers an interesting view of collaborative hierarchy. The context for this particular narrative is the role of arbitrator into which Moses was thrust as the leader of the Israelites. Because of the enormous number of people and the understandably high number of disputes, Moses spent most of his day settling these disputes. The very fact that people brought these decisions to Moses indicates that there was a decision-making hierarchy at work. When Moses' father-in-law, Jethro, saw the dynamics of the situation, he offered this wise counsel to his son-in-law, "What you are doing is not good. You and these people who come to you will only wear yourselves out. The work is too heavy for you; you cannot handle it alone. Listen now to me and I will give you some advice, and may God be with you."[12]

Jethro's advice focused primarily on enlisting other capable men to serve as judges and appointing them as officials over thousands, hundreds, fifties and tens. Jethro recommended a hierarchical structure where judges have responsibility for as few as ten individuals. In addition, a kind of appeals court would be established where judges would have judiciary oversight over other judges and deal with more difficult cases. The most difficult cases would then be brought to Moses. Jethro counseled, "Have them serve as judges for the people at all times, but have them bring every difficult case to you; the simple cases they can decide themselves."[13]

Jethro advised Moses to put in place a very hierarchical structure with Moses clearly positioned at the top. It was also collaborative in the sense that the process of distinguishing simple cases from more difficult ones would necessarily require collaboration between Moses and the other designated leaders. Moses' response to Jethro's counsel adds another collaborative dimension to this narrative. After all, Moses was the one in charge. He was the one who God had called and placed in this position of leadership. Moses should have known best what structures were needed to make good decisions. How did Moses respond? He listened: "Moses listened to his father-in-law and did everything he said."[14] It is clear that Moses owned the decision concerning what would be the best structure. The decision did not belong to Jethro *and* Moses. It was Moses' decision, yet, Moses was wise enough to include his father-in-law in the collaborative process.

Decisions About Direction

The argument, perhaps, could be made that the only reason Moses willingly collaborated in Exodus 18 was because the person offering counsel was his father-in-law. However, this same collaborative hierarchy appears in Numbers 10. A very clear hierarchical structure existed among the Israelites. The Israelites were organized by division, and each division had a person in command. Nethanel son of Zuar was over the division of the tribe of Issachar. Eliab son of Helon was over the division of the tribe of Zebulun. Abidan son of Gideoni was over the division of the tribe of Benjamin, and so on. Everything was very ordered, and each division had specific responsibilities when the Israelites would relocate.

In this particular narrative, the Israelites set out from the Desert of Sinai and eventually settled in the Desert of Paran. The movement of the Israelites was guided "at the Lord's command through Moses."[15] To aid in movement from location to location, God provided a cloud during the day and a pillar of fire at night. On the surface, the decisions concerning the movement and relocation of the Israelites seem to be made in isolation. God directed Moses, and Moses told everyone else what God revealed to him. The text, however, points to a more collaborative decision-making process. Moses' strong desire that Horab not depart from the Israelites and return to his own land and his own people reveals this collaborative work. Horab was, apparently, giving counsel to Moses concerning where the Israelites should establish their camp. "Moses said, 'Please do not leave us. You know where we should camp in the desert, and you can be our eyes. If you come with us, we will share with you whatever good things the LORD gives us."[16]

God led the Israelites through the desert, and the decisions concerning where the Israelites should camp were ultimately entrusted to Moses. However, Moses did not make these decisions in isolation. He sought input from Horab. Again, just as in his relationship with Jethro, Moses functioned in a collaborative way in his decision making.

Moses and the Leaders of the Community

The collaborative hierarchy embodied in Moses' actions was not limited to singular voices. In other words, Moses did not only collaborate with one other person such as Jethro or Horab. Scripture shows Moses collaborating with other leaders in the community. Over and over again in the book of Numbers people came to Moses seeking a decision. And while, ultimately, it was Moses who rendered the final decision, he was not alone in the process. He did not isolate himself in decision making.

In many cases, questions requiring the rendering of a decision were addressed not only to Moses but also to key leaders who surrounded him. Numbers 32 offers one of many examples. The Reubanites and the Gadites wanted a portion of the land that God had given the Israelites. They had a great deal of livestock and wanted land that was suitable for sustaining their herds and flocks. Particularly, they wanted the lands of Jazer and Gilead. The final decision on the distribution of the land seems to belong to Moses. Moses, however, was not alone in the decision-making process. He had surrounded himself with a group of individuals who appear to have had some sort of collaborative role in the decisions. The text identifies the group as consisting of Eleazar and other leaders of the community.

When the Reubanites and Gadites sought a decision on the matter, they brought it to the entire group: "So they came to Moses and Eleazar the priest and to the leaders of the community, and said ' . . . the land the LORD subdued before the people of Israel—are suitable for livestock, and your servants have livestock. If we have found favor in your eyes,' they said, 'let this land be given to your servants as our possession. Do not make us cross the Jordan.'"[17] The presence of Eleazar and the leaders of the community did not mean, however, that this was a group decision made by consensus. Unlike the Acts 15 decision, the Numbers 32 text does not reveal the discussion that may have occurred between Moses, Eleazar, and the other leaders prior to a decision being made. The text does show that Moses ultimately rendered the decision: "Then Moses said to them '...if all of you will go armed over the Jordan before the LORD until he has driven his enemies out before him— then when the land is subdued before the LORD, you may return and be free from your obligation to the LORD and to Israel. And this land will be your possession before the LORD.'"[18] He then continued on to clarify the consequences that would occur if they failed to function in this way. This is collaborative hierarchy at its best.

Joshua and the Leaders of the Community

Moses was not the only Old Testament leader to reflect a decision-making ethos that could be described as collaborative hierarchy. In fact, the person who replaced Moses as the leader of the Israelites, Joshua, functioned in much the same way. In Joshua 17, Joshua was also asked to make a decision concerning land allocation. Zelophehad had no sons, only daughters. Their names were Mahlah, Noah, Hoglah, Milcah and Tirzah. Women were typically not the recipients of the inheritance of the father. In this case, however, they believed that they should each receive a portion of the land that had been promised to their father. Even though Joshua owned the decision, the same group of leaders who surrounded Moses surrounded him. This group's involvement in the decision-making process is evidenced by the fact that the five daughters brought their request to the entire group. It reads, "They went to Eleazar the priest, Joshua son of Nun, and the leaders and said, 'The LORD commanded Moses to give us an inheritance among our brothers.'"[19] Joshua, however, rendered the decision. "So Joshua gave them an inheritance along with the brothers of their father, according to the LORD's command."[20]

Decisions and the
Minority Report

Collaborative hierarchy is more than listening to and agreeing with the loudest voices. Moses' decision concerning the taking of the land God had promise to His people offers an excellent example. About a year after the Israelites fled the bondage of Egypt, they found themselves poised to enter the Promised Land and take possession of that which God had said was theirs. Before Moses made the decision to enter the land, he sent out spies to survey the situation and bring him a report. This was collaborative hierarchy in action. Moses owned the decision, however, he was willing to invite others into the conversation. In Numbers 13 Moses sent out twelve people to explore the land of Canaan. When they returned, the recommendations from the twelve were not the same. The majority opinion was that the land was rich and bountiful but that the people who already resided there were powerful and lived in very large, fortified cities. The recommendation of the majority was to not try to take possession of the land. They were convinced that any attempt to do so would end in defeat. Their counsel is reflected in the statement, "We seemed like grasshoppers in our own eyes, and we looked the same to them."[21]

Caleb and Joshua, however, presented a minority report that offered different counsel: "Caleb silenced the people before Moses and said, 'We should go up and take possession of the land, for we can certainly do it.'"[22] Seen from the perspective of history, the counsel offered by the minority was the best counsel. Moses, however, ignored it and made a decision that reflected the counsel of the majority. In so doing, he ignored the promises of God and failed to seize the opportunity God had provided. The results were disastrous, and Israel spent the next thirty-nine years in the desert before it had the opportunity to once again enter into the land. Moses died before that opportunity came and never entered the Promised Land.

The use of collaborative hierarchy does not automatically result in good decisions. The decision-maker still must determine what weight to place on the counsel he or she receives from others. The collaborative process consists of more than weighing public opinion and then making a decision embraced by the majority. The process involves gaining insight and perspective that informs the decision but does not determine it.

A Day of Terror

In Ezekiel 7, the prophet warned Israel of an impending judgment. Ezekiel painted an incredibly vivid picture of these coming future events. He spoke of terror and the absence of peace. Calamity would befall the people. A sense of fear would be driven by unfounded rumors that were allowed to take root in the hearts of the people. He said, "The king will mourn, the prince will be clothed with despair, and the hands of the people of the land will tremble. I will deal with them according to their conduct, and by their own standards I will judge them. Then they will know that I am the LORD."[23] The prophet did not paint a pleasant future. He prophesied about a time of judgment and justice.

One consequence of this judgment—the removal of vision and wise counsel—was directed toward leaders in general, kings specifically: The text reads, "They will try to get a vision from the prophet; the teaching of the law by the priest will be lost, as will the counsel of the elders."[24] Scripture implies that even the king, the person empowered to make any and all decisions, needed wise counsel in order to rule rightly and with justice. Even the king needed to be a part of a decision-making ethos that is collaborative. When wise counsel is removed, so is the ability to make the kind of decisions that reflect God's mercy and justice and that provide for the needs of the community.

It was a day of terror, indeed, and it is one that every pastor should avoid. The sad reality is that some pastors choose to remove the counsel of the elders. Empowered by hierarchy, these pastors create a decision-making ethos void of collaboration and in doing so isolate themselves from the very resources God has provided for good decision making.

Chapter Summary

While the Bible may not make a clear and distinct case for any particular form of church polity or decision-making structure, there does seem to be a decision-making ethos that emerges in scripture that reflects collaborative hierarchy. In Acts 15, James collaborated with many leaders, including Paul, Barnabas, and Peter, before making a decision concerning circumcision and the Gentile believers. Though there appears to be no consensus before James made his decision, either among the leaders or the church at large, both groups enthusiastically embraced the decision.

In the Old Testament, Moses and Joshua sought the counsel of others before making decisions on such wide-ranging issues as judicial review, wilderness campsites, property rights, and taking possession of the land God had promised. The embracing of collaborative hierachy does not autmatically result in good decisions. The reality of conflicting counsel means that the decision maker still must determine what weight to place on the counsel he or she receives from others.

7 | How Vision is Formed

L OCAL CONGREGATIONS TEND TO VIEW THE FORMATION of vision in two ways. Some view vision as something that is resident within the people God has placed within a congregation, and it *emerges from* the congregation. Others view vision as resident primarily within the leader God has placed in the congregation, and it is *confirmed by* the congregation.

When a congregation believes that vision emerges from within itself, then their goal becomes to create a congregational process through which that vision can emerge. In many congregations, this process takes the form of visioning meetings, retreats or conferences that involve the staff and a select segment of the congregation. This group brainstorms and carefully records ideas. Common themes are identified. Ideas that seem to garner the broadest interest are advanced, while those ideas that generate little interest are usually discarded. Eventually, through a highly guided process, ideas emerge that are viewed as reflective of God's vision for the congregation.

Some consulting firms who specialize in consulting local congregations have designed their entire business model around the idea that vision emerges from the congregation. One consulting firm focuses on discovering the DNA of a particular congregation. They assume that the DNA resides within the congregation, and vision formation is merely a process of discovering it. This process builds consensus and, in the short-term, often leaves the congregation feeling good about the vision that has emerged. The longer-term results are less conclusive.

The theological underpinning for this approach is typically rooted in the work of the Holy Spirit. Participants reason that since the Holy Spirit is at work in the life of every member of the congregation, the vision for the congregation is something that should emerge from the congregation itself. The process, however, rarely remains consistent with this theological conviction. In most congregations, visioning does not include the entire congregation but rather a select number of members. In all but the smallest of congregations, including the entire congregation in the process is generally viewed as cumbersome and impractical.

Another View of Vision Formation

Another view of vision formation within the local congregation suggests that vision is generally given to a leader and then confirmed by the congregation. Some are hesitant to embrace this view of vision formation out of a concern that it can lead to isolated leaders who impose their subjective view of God's leading on the congregation with little regard for the insights of the community as a whole. There are, no doubt, plenty of examples to which people can point where this has occurred; however, isolation and individualism are not inevitable. Within the context of a collaborative hierarchy, it is possible for vision to emerge from the leader and at the same time not marginalize the community in the process.

Scripture offers some wonderful examples of this process. Numbers 12 details a conflict that took place between Miriam, Aaron, and Moses. The conflict focused on vision formation. Miriam and Aaron questioned some of the decisions Moses had made, particularly his decision to marry a Cushite wife. Their questions about this particular decision led to broader questions concerning Moses' role in articulating God's vision for the people of Israel. Miriam and Aaron argued that since God had spoken to them as well as to Moses, they should be equally involved in the formation and declaration of vision: "'Has the LORD spoken only through Moses?' they asked. 'Hasn't he also spoken through us?'"[1]

This argument continues to be made in local congregations today. Does the fact that the voice of God is alive and
active in the lives of many persons within the community
mean that vision should emerge from the community rather
than from a particular individual within the community?
God's response to Miriam and Aaron suggest otherwise.
God responded to this conflict by telling Moses, Aaron,
and Miriam to go to the Tent of Meeting. God came to
them there in a pillar of cloud and told Aaron and Miriam
to step forward.

> He said, "Listen to my words: When a
> prophet of the LORD is among you, I
> reveal myself to him in visions, I speak
> to him in dreams. But this is not true
> of my servant Moses; he is faithful in
> all my house. With him I speak face
> to face, clearly and not in riddles; he
> sees the form of the LORD. Why then
> were you not afraid to speak against my
> servant Moses?" The anger of the LORD
> burned against them, and he left them.[2]

It would be a mistake to equate the way that God spoke
to Moses with the way that God speaks to the senior pastor
of a local congregation. It would also be a mistake to equate
the role of the senior pastor of a local congregation to the
role that Moses played in the life of Israel. Moses played
a unique role in the biblical narrative, and God spoke to
him in a unique way. There does, however, seem to be
some themes that emerge from this narrative that revolve
around the important role that leadership plays in the midst

of community.

It seems that God often places the mantle of leadership on specific individuals within the midst of community and then guides the community utilizing these individuals in unique ways. The focus of this narrative is not that senior pastors are just like Moses, but rather it suggests that God used Moses to give direction to the community of Israel in a different way compared to others in the community. God spoke in and through others in the community, but the way in which God spoke to Moses was unique and enabled Moses to provide visionary leadership. This does not mean that vision formation should be an isolated process, nor should leaders claim such intimate communication with God that collaboration is minimized or avoided. The narrative seems to suggest, however, that the clarifying of direction for a community of faith, or for a sub-group within that community, can emerge from individuals who have been identified as leaders.

Vision Formation and the Apostles' Teaching

What about vision formation in the New Testament? Is it profoundly different from vision formation accounts in the Old Testament and the narrative of Moses? Does the age of Pentecost and the outpouring of God's Spirit on all those within the community necessitate a different view on how vision is formed? Acts 2 offers an interesting look at leadership and vision formation in the early church. Peter

126 Free to Lead

plays a significant role in this narrative, which focuses on
the historical fulfillment of the coming of the Holy Spirit.
As the events of Acts 2 unfold, vision formation in this
community of faith is modeled in a powerful way.

Peter did three things that are crucial to vision
formation. First, he defined reality. When the day of
Pentecost came, this community of believers experienced a
number of very unusual manifestations of the Holy Spirit:
"Suddenly a sound like the blowing of a violent wind came
from heaven and filled the whole house where they were
sitting. They saw what seemed to be tongues of fire that
separated and came to rest on each of them. All of them
were filled with the Holy Spirit and began to speak in other
tongues as the Spirit enabled them."[3] The manifestations
of the Holy Spirit frightened and confused many who were
present. Some made light of what was happening. Peter
helped them understand the reality of what they were expe-
riencing and to place it within the context of that which had
been prophesied by Joel: "In the last days, God says, I will
pour out my Spirit on all people. Your sons and daughters
will prophesy, your young men will see visions, your old
men will dream dreams. Even on my servants, both men
and women, I will pour out my Spirit in those days, and
they will prophesy."[4]

Secondly, Peter proclaimed the gospel. He clearly
explained who Christ is, what he had done and how they
could respond: "'God has made this Jesus, whom you
crucified, both Lord and Christ.' When the people heard
this, they were cut to the heart and said to Peter and the

other apostles, 'Brothers, what shall we do?' Peter replied, 'Repent and be baptized, every one of you, in the name of Jesus Christ for the forgiveness of your sins. And you will receive the gift of the Holy Spirit'"[5]

Thirdly, Peter, along with the rest of the Apostles, continued to proclaim the practical implications of the gospel to this newly formed community, and it appears that the vision for this new community began to take shape around that teaching: "They devoted themselves to the apostles' teaching and to the fellowship, to the breaking of bread and to prayer."[6] Acts 2:42-47 shows a community living out a vision that seems to be formed around the Apostles' teaching. It was a community defined by joy, praise, rich table fellowship, an invitational life-style, evangelism, and radical generosity. People were willing to sell some of their possessions and give to anyone who had need. The result of this compelling vision was that the, "Lord added to their number daily those who were being saved."[7]

Acts 2 describes a community of believers, filled with the Holy Spirit, with a singular sense of vision and mission. It does not appear that each Spirit-filled believer cast his or her own individual vision nor did vision simply emerge from the community through some type of consensus building process. Rather, the vision seems to have formed around the Apostles' teaching.

If one views congregational vision as something that is formed primarily around the Apostles' teaching (now manifest in canonized scripture), then the pulpit is as important, or perhaps even more important, than the boardroom in vision formation. Often, local congregations attempt to separate the Apostles' teaching from vision formation. They view the preaching of the Word as that which takes place on the weekend in the midst of worship, and they view vision formation as that which takes place in the middle of the week in boards, committees, and visioning conferences. Though rarely articulated, preaching and vision formation often are seen as separate and distinct functions in the local congregation.

To separate preaching from vision formation, however, is to misunderstand both. When the gospel is clearly proclaimed in a local congregation, vision is formed. Whether it is formalized or not, the vision of a local congregation is shaped each week through the Apostles' teaching. Obviously, this doesn't mean that detailed plans and programs should first be introduced from the pulpit, before there has been the opportunity for dialogue and collaboration. Mark Batterson learned that lesson quickly at National Community Church: "Early on I mentioned things in sermons I hadn't communicated to the inner circles. That was a mistake."[8] The role of the pulpit in vision formation must not be used as a means of avoiding necessary and important conversations concerning the direction of a local congregation. Neither should it limit brainstorming sessions out of which creative ideas for implementing vision are produced. Preaching does, however, provide a framework in which those conversations can take place.

The connection between vision formation and preaching can make it difficult to have more than one primary preaching pastor in a local congregation. A local congregation utilizing multiple services or multiple campuses where each service or each campus has its own preaching pastor may find the pursuit of a common vision extremely challenging.

Prior to the technological and sociological changes that made it possible to utilize video to provide the same sermon at multiple campus locations, very few congregations operated multiple campuses. Technological advances now allow congregations to have multiple locations, sometimes even in multiple cities, with multiple styles of worship and yet still utilize the same preaching pastor. A proliferation of multi-site congregations has resulted. There are now more than 3,000 multi-site churches in the United States.[9] This is a large increase over just ten years ago. Sometimes multi-site congregations do utilize different preaching pastors at each campus. However, unlike the utilization of video, the practice often results in multiple congregations with multiple visions masquerading as one congregation.

Vision Formation in the Congregations Surveyed

All five senior pastors who were surveyed for this book reflected the view that vision resides primarily within the leaders God has placed in the congregation and then the congregation confirms that vision. Harry Kuehl talks about the importance of other leaders being involved in this process of vision confirmation, "Jeanette (lead pastor) and I take what we believe is the vision that God has given us on any particular issue, and we will share that with the management team and have the pastors affirm or not affirm whether they believe that this is of God."[10] Kuehl expands further on the importance of having vision confirmed by others in the congregation, "I'm able to set forth what I believe is the direction that comes from God, but I can trust if it's truly from the Lord, the Holy Spirit will create that same sense in the heart of others. Through that dialogue we can begin to see if what has come to the surface in my heart is really coming from God."[11] This collaborative process avoids the individualism and isolationism that can often characterize strong, visionary leaders.

Concerning the role of the congregation in embracing the vision of leadership, Kuehl talks about the importance of trust, "We have not given our congregation cause to question the leadership style we have, which is vision coming from the top down and then embraced and implemented by the broader congregation. I believe the point at which we betray the congregation's trust and love, our leadership style wouldn't be as effective as it is."[12] Trust is the currency of visionary leaders. Without trust, motives are questioned, and vision will be not embraced. Some congregations hesitate to embrace visionary leaders because trust has been broken, either by the current leader or some past leader. This may be one of the reasons that pastors who have been at one congregation over a long period of time are able to experience such visional momentum. They have established a culture of trust within the congregation that results in a willingness to embrace and affirm vision.

A leader-driven approach to vision formation does not assume that the leadership of the church simply articulates the vision, and the congregation automatically accepts it. Often times, the process of embracing the vision takes time. Steve Treash talks about the importance of patience in vision formation, "I think, even in forming vision, you have to be patient. The leader needs to read the group he or she is leading. A leader can be a strong visionary and still take a longer view. Taking a longer view allows time, God's Spirit, teaching, and relational development to bring the congregation to the same place but at a slightly different pace."[13] Treash also talks about the way in which vision is communicated to the congregation, "I'd say that the leadership of the church primarily discerns the vision and then in a measured process teaches the raw material behind the vision so that when the vision is presented the congregation has the spiritual understanding of the raw material."[14] What Treash refers to as the "raw material" is the Apostles' teaching, the biblical framework out of which the specificity of the vision arises. Again, vision formation and preaching retain a distinct connectedness.

Gideon Thompson has a very strong view on how vision is formed in the local congregation. His view of vision formation is informed by Habakkuk 2, "Habakkuk prayed and God gave him a vision to write down. So I seek what the Lord wants. It's not my kingdom come; it's thy kingdom come. He's the one that's building the church. So I really need to get a vision from God as to what our emphasis should be in the city of Boston. I need to hear from the Spirit."[15] Thompson goes on to reflect on what he sees as the unique role of the senior pastor in vision formation, "We recognize there is a 'Moses' in the house. I'm that person, and so I'm responsible for fasting and praying and hearing from God about the vision and direction. Other men and women in leadership in our congregation also fast and pray and are responsible in a similar way in their area of responsibility."[16]

Even a congregation like Jubilee Christian Church that has very strong visionary leadership, employs a collaborative nature to the formation of vision. Thompson talks about the coming together of the members of the pastoral staff to talk about vision, "The four of us get together regularly to talk about the overall projection of where we see ourselves going and what we hear the Lord saying to each of us. All of us are praying and seeking the face of God. They hear me because they know I have a responsibility as the head. But I hear them, too."[17] Thompson is an excellent example of the importance of collaboration, especially within a ministry context that views vision as resident primarily within the leader God has placed in the congregation. When the leader is not collaborative, vision formation easily becomes isolated. Chapter 8 will explore the dangers of isolation, not only in the formation of vision, but also in the decision making that is a part of the normal operations of an organization.

Chapter Summary

Vision formation in congregational life is often viewed in one of two ways. It is either viewed as being primarily resident within the congregation and *emerging from* the congregation or as primarily resident within the leader and *confirmed by* the congregation. While there is no definitive biblical position on vision formation, there are biblical examples that would suggest that the clarifying direction for the community of faith often emerges from individual leaders within the community and is then confirmed by the community. The congregations who were surveyed for this book had a similar view. In this paradigm, trust is the currency of visionary leaders. Without it, motives are questioned, and vision will not be embraced. Even in the context of strong, visionary leadership, there still needs to be a collaborative nature to vision formation in order to avoid isolation and individualism. Additionally, there is a close connection between vision formation and the Apostles' teaching. The implication being that the pulpit is at least as important as the boardroom in forming vision.

8 | The Deadly Effect of Isolation

SEVERAL YEARS AGO, DR. ASHISH NANDA SPOKE AT the Willow Creek Association's annual Leadership Summit. I had the privilege of being in attendance and hearing Dr. Nanda's presentation. Dr. Nanda is currently a professor at the Harvard Business School, and a member of Harvard's Negotiations, Organizations, and Markets faculty team. Some of his recent research focused on determining the impact upon organizations when they go outside of the organization to hire "stars." Nanda describes a star as someone who has already experienced significant success within a particular organization. His research focused on stock analysts because it was easy to quantify success and because the job description of a stock analyst does not change significantly when he or she moves from one company to another. His research produced the following conclusions.

1. The performance of a star tends to go down after he or she moves from one organization to the next.

2. The performance of the people in the new organization who work with the star tends to go down after the star arrives.

3. The stock market tends to react negatively to the organization that hired the star. In other words, when a company announces that it has hired a star, the stock price of that company tends to go down.

Based on his research, Nanda believes the primary cause for this downward trend in performance relates to issues of integration. He indicates that 90 percent of the success that a star may have in a new organization is the result of post-hiring integration. Companies that were able to hire entire teams from another organization performed better than those who just hired the star of the team.[1]

While the local congregation is a vastly different kind of organization than an investment firm, and pastors have very different roles than stock analysts, Nanda's research offers a tangible way to measure the negative impact of isolation. His research highlights one of the benefits of collaborative hierarchy. Collaborative hierarchy tends to result in better decision making. Stars who were separated from their teams performed at a lower level than those who remained integrated into their teams. The isolation of the star from the team resulted in poorer decision making.

In the local congregation, it is harder to quantify poor

decision making. Decisions are often very subjective, and it is difficult to measure their impact. Nanda's findings do, however, hint at a principle that may apply, regardless of the organization. The isolation of the leader of an organization or of a department within an organization tends to result in poorer decisions. The answer, however, is not to dismantle the hierarchy or do away with the role of the leader, but rather to function in a more integrated, collaborative way.

Overcoming Generational Isolation

Leaders in today's world must engage those around them in order to lead effectively. This is certainly true for congregational leaders. In local congregations, isolation often occurs in the area of generational differences. In strictly hierarchical organizations, those at or near the top of the organizational chart are often persons from the same generation. Younger leaders who are further down the organizational chart sometimes are isolated from those who have positional authority. Effective leaders must bridge these generational differences. When younger leaders present new ideas or different strategies, those who are presently in power often view them as threatening. When younger leaders are excluded from the decision-making process, they often view the individuals in positions of power as obstacles to missional success. These perspectives result in an inevitable competition between generations. The older generation fights to hold onto its power, while the younger generation works to move those presently in leadership to the sidelines.

This generational competition is more pronounced in an organization that is strictly hierarchical. A collaborative hierarchy that enjoys a more familial model offers a very different paradigm. Healthy families are not characterized by generational competition. Parents are not in competition with their children, and grandparents are not in competition with their grandchildren. Instead, each generation focuses on encouraging and empowering the next generation. Relational connectedness within the family reinforces the reality that the differences between generations may not be as big as they at first appear. The differences that are present become opportunities for dialogue and mutual learning. The younger generation learns from the wisdom and experiences of those who have journeyed for a little longer. The older generation learns from the wisdom and experiences of those who are able to look at old issues through a fresh new lens.

Organizations that employ a collaborative hierarchy often are able to leverage generational differences in a way that benefits the organization. Instead of battling for power, leaders engage in sharing power. Older leaders look for ways to empower younger leaders. This approach is not about simply changing where people are on the organizational chart or removing older leaders from positional power and replacing them with younger leaders. Collaborative hierarchy means developing a culture of relational connectedness within the organization, so people are empowered to lead, regardless of where they are on the organizational chart.

Collaborative hierarchy seems to be reflective of the kind of leadership for which an emerging, postmodern generation is looking. Our culture is increasingly wary of the "organized church." This is especially true among young adults. Organizations that are characterized by rigid, hierarchical structures, where isolated leaders hand down their decisions from on high, do not appeal to an emerging generation.

In his book, *Leadership Next*, Eddie Gibbs takes a comprehensive look at the various leadership issues that he believes must be addressed if church leaders are going to be effective in a postmodern, pluralistic environment. Gibbs defines a Christian leader as "a person with a God-given capacity and the God-given responsibility to influence a specific group of God's people toward God's purpose for the group."[2] According to Gibbs, leadership is all about relationships. The ability of pastors to influence their staff and their congregation grows out of the quality and character of the relationship they maintain with both. This is especially true with those under thirty-five years of age. He says, "Younger adults are walking away from those institutions characterized by a culture of control and a style of delegation that is considered disempowering."[3]

Emerging leaders desire to be a part of organizations where relationships are highly valued, and their skills are effectively utilized to accomplish the mission of the organization. Organizations where a strict hierarchy results in the isolation of those at the top of the hierarchy magnify generational differences. Organizations that reflect a more collaborative hierarchy minimize these differences. Local congregations whose decision-making ethos reflects collaborative hierarchy often are able to keep emerging leaders on staff for a longer period of time because they are involved in the organization in a more meaningful way.

Diversity at the Table

There is no greater metaphor for family connectedness than the kitchen table. Families gather around the table to share a common meal, tell stories, laugh together, and even make decisions. If a family member is missing from the table they miss out on much of what it means to be a part of the family.

In organizations, the family table is represented by the discussions that take place out of which decisions are made. It is extremely important who is at the table. In strictly hierarchical organizations, very few people are at the table. Very few people have the opportunity to offer their input on important decisions. Not only is the number of people at the table small, but everyone at the table often looks the same. They have similar backgrounds and similar experiences. They may be the same gender, ethnicity, and age. In other words, there is not much diversity at the table. This is a loss for any organization. However, when the organization is a local congregation, it is an even greater loss. Sameness at the table limits perspective in making decisions. A richness occurs when diversity is at the table. Diversity does create challenges, but even these challenges can be leveraged into positives.

In his book, *Where the Nations Meet*, Stephen A. Rhodes denotes the benefits of dealing with cultural differences in the context of the church. He believes the challenges of dealing with these cultural differences are actually part of the process of better understanding who believers are in Christ. He says, "Cross-cultural interaction is not only the good, tolerant, and open-minded thing to do as Christians, but it is also the means by which we may discover our full identity as the children of God."[4] While Rhodes' focuses primarily on ethnic diversity, the same principles also apply when dealing with other differences such as age, gender, giftedness, and personality. Diversity at the table enriches perspective and enables decisions to be made that are not limited by cultural bias.

Diversity at the table reflects the rich potential of collaborative hierarchy. A certain degree of diversity is built into every family. When the family gathers around the table, it includes young and old, male and female. There is also a diversity of gifts, talents, passions and personalities. Healthy families embrace this diversity and seek to affirm every member of the family regardless of differences. Healthy organizations do the same. They strive to make sure there is diversity at the table so that the decision-making process is not limited to people who look and think alike. By nurturing a decision-making ethos that reflects the diversity of the congregation, leaders become more aware of other perspectives. Their decisions, therefore, are better informed and more sensitive to this rich diversity of people.

Loss of Missional Momentum

In his book, *How The Mighty Fall—And Why Some Companies Never Give In*, Jim Collins provides an interesting look at the contributing factors that led to the demise of once highly successful companies. These companies made the transition from good to great and were able to sustain growth over a significant period of time. Eventually, however, these companies failed. Collins contrasts the trajectory of these companies with the trajectory of other companies in the same industry, over the same period of time, facing many of the same external influences, and yet able to continue to thrive. Based on his research, Collins identifies "five stages of death" that were present in the companies that failed but were not present in the companies that continued to thrive.[5]

- Stage #1 is the "hubris born of success." In each case, the companies that failed experienced tremendous success early on. The success manifested itself in rapidly expanding human and financial resources. It seemed as if everything the company did was successful. However, rapid growth and extraordinary resources minimized the importance of careful discernment in decision making.

- Stage #2 is the "undisciplined pursuit of growth." In almost every case, the eventual failure of the company was not rooted in complacency, but in overreaching. In the pursuit of rapid growth, decisions were made that moved the company beyond its core competencies and away from its core values and ethos.

- Stage #3 is the "denial of risk and peril." The positives of the organization were constantly highlighted, and the negatives were minimized. Leadership rationalized warning signs that the organization was in trouble, often pointing to a myriad of outside circumstances as the cause. The decision-making culture of the organization was rarely questioned.

- Stage #4 is the "grasping for salvation." When the decline of the organization was too obvious to ignore, there was the hope that the organization was just one or two "game-changing" decisions away from turning the ship around. This unhealthy decision-making culture usually hastened the demise that the organization was desperately trying to avoid.

- Stage #5 is the "capitulation to irrelevance or death." When this stage was reached, there was little hope for the organization to rebound. Death with dignity was the best possible outcome.

Each of the five stages that Collins identifies can be found in local congregations. In the church, the conversation of organizational death is generally reserved for small congregations that are facing near-term survival issues. Large congregations rarely think in terms of these five stages. However, large congregations that have already experienced significant growth are most susceptible to the stages Collins describes.

In the context of the local congregation, where faith is often equated with risk taking, the undisciplined pursuit of growth can easily become spiritualized. Churches that have experienced significant growth over a short period of time often are tempted to take risks that result in the overreaching of both financial and human resources. They develop a kind of success entitlement mentality that assumes future growth at the same pace, or an even faster pace, than in the past. This perspective leads to decisions that are undisciplined at best and reckless at worst. The denial of risk and the grasping for salvation often follow. The result is a loss of missional momentum that may never be regained.

The isolation of the decision makers at the top of the hierarchy is frequently a contributing factor. Whether it is the CEO of a large company or the senior pastor of a large congregation, the five stages of death that Collins describes are easier to move through if the leader remains isolated. Highly gifted, articulate leaders are perhaps the most susceptible. Their ability to reframe reality through compelling communication makes it easier to be in denial and to convince others that everything is just fine. The fact that pastors are given a platform each week to interpret the reality of what is happening, makes them even more susceptible. Even meetings where all the right players are at the table can become functionally isolated if the pastor uses the filibuster of rhetoric to shape the discussion and minimize genuine dialogue.

The isolation of the leader often results in a kind of pride that lures the leader into believing that he or she has all of the answers. Several of the senior pastors surveyed for this book spoke about the isolating impact of pride. Mark Batterson reflected on the danger of overvaluing one's own perspective, "The leader needs to stay humble. The moment you think you have a 360° perspective, blind spots will be formed that hinder the growth of organization."[6] It is an unwillingness to allow themselves to become isolated that has helped each of the six churches surveyed for this book avoid the fives stages of death described by Collins and experience sustained, long-term growth.

Isolation and the Washington Redskins

Two examples, one from scripture and one from the world of sports, illustrate the damaging effect of isolation. In 2009 the Washington Redskins paid an incredible amount of money to acquire defensive tackle Albert Haynesworth from the Tennessee Titans. Haynesworth was an All-Pro defensive lineman who many people thought would dramatically improve the defense of the Redskins.

He has not and the reason may be surprising. It is not that Haynesworth lacks talent or that his skills have diminished significantly. In fact, he is an incredibly gifted athlete. The reason has to do with the decision-making ethos of the Washington Redskins.

Daniel Snyder owns the Redskins. The decision-making structure of the organization is clearly hierarchical. As the owner, Snyder is the ultimate decision maker in most player personnel decisions. However, he often makes decisions with little or no input from others in the organization. The acquisition of Albert Haynesworth is a prime example. Haynesworth is most effective in a defensive scheme that allows for a great deal of improvising on the part of the defensive linemen. Over the last decade, the Redskins have run a very disciplined defensive scheme that requires its defensive linemen to not improvise. They remain committed to such a system. Had Snyder sought the input of a broader group within the organization, particularly those who run the defense, he would have either decided not to acquire Haynesworth or would have insisted that the defensive scheme was changed to leverage Haynesworth's enormous talent. Unfortunately, neither decision was made, which left the Redskins with a very high-priced defensive lineman who was both frustrated and ineffective. In 2011, after many attempts to make the acquisition work, Haynesworth was released from the Washington Redskins.

This example from the world of sports illustrates a profound point. The health of any organization, even the performance-driven environment of a professional football team, rises and falls on the health of its decision-making ethos. If those entrusted with decisions choose to make decisions in an isolated fashion, the organization will suffer. It doesn't take a great deal of insight to recognize that some of the most successful organizations in the NFL over the last decade have a decision-making ethos that reflects collaborative hierarchy. Leaders are clearly empowered to make decisions, but there is a great deal of collaboration involved to insure that each decision and each player fits into the larger scheme of the organization.

Isolation and the King

The second example comes from the narrative of scripture. The text of 2 Chronicles 25 provides a very interesting look into what happens when a leader acts in isolation. Amaziah was the king of Judah. He was twenty-five years old when he became the king, and he reigned for twenty-nine years. His reign was profoundly impacted by the degree to which he was collaborative in his decision making. In the early years of his reign, he was more collaborative. One of the first things he did as king was to bring together all of the young men in Judah who were ready for military service. That number was 300,000 men. It was a large army, but Amaziah believed it was not large enough. So he hired an additional 100,000 men from Israel and paid them. This decision was not wise. However, because he had surrounded himself with some Godly individuals who he allowed to speak into his life, he was willing to reconsider his decision and avoid disaster. Scripture reads, "A man of God came to him and said, 'O king, these troops from Israel must not march with you, for the LORD is not with Israel—not with any of the people of Ephraim. Even if you go and fight courageously in battle, God will overthrow you before the enemy, for God has the power to help or to overthrow.'"[7] Amaziah listened to the counsel of this man and sent home the troops who had come from Ephraim. The result was that Amaziah was successful in his military pursuits.

Later in his reign, however, Amaziah ignored the counsel of a prophet who warned him about the foreign gods Amaziah had set up in Jerusalem. Not only did he ignore the counsel of the prophet, he isolated himself from godly counsel by surrounding himself with ungodly advisors. Amaziah was so isolated in his leadership that he even ignored the counsel of Jehoash, king of Israel. Amaziah was intent on going into battle against Jehoash, a battle he would surely lose, and Jehoash warned him so. But Amaziah was completely isolated in his decision making and ignored everyone except for his closest advisors. The result was devastating. Judah was routed. Amaziah was captured. The wall of Jerusalem was broken down. The gold, silver, and other priceless items were taken from the temple and the palace. Amaziah turned away completely from following the Lord. Finally, he fled Jerusalem but was hunted down and killed.

While the effects of isolation are certainly not as

dramatic in local congregations as they were for Amaziah and Judah, they are deadly nonetheless. They often result in poor decisions that undermine missional momentum, create financial crises, marginalize emerging leadership, or create unnecessary conflict. Collaborative hierarchy, on the other hand, creates a culture in which the most insightful and most trusted talent of the organization is invited to the table when important decisions are being considered. The collaborative process does not undermine the positional authority of the leader. Quite the contrary, it enables the leader to make the best possible decision, even on matters that may not reflect his or her expertise. This is so important because no leader, regardless of giftedness or position held within the organization, holds all of the necessary information and insight to make the healthy, timely decisions on every issue for which he or she is responsible.

Chapter Summary

The isolation of the leader of an organization can result in poorer decision making. Collaborative hierarchies that are familial in nature tend to minimize generational differences that can often isolate the leader from emerging leaders in the organization. Organizations that are characterized by rigid, hierarchical structures where isolated leaders hand down their decisions from on high do not appeal to an emerging generation. Diversity at the table in regards to race, age, gender, gifts, talents, and passions often results in decisions that are better informed and more sensitive to the diversity that exists within the organization. The isolation of the leader can make the organization more susceptible to decline. Examples from arenas as wide ranging as the world of sports and the Old Testament illustrate the damaging impact of isolation on leaders and the organizations they lead.

9 | Nurturing Collaborative Hierarchy

IN HIS BOOK, *Leading Without Power: Finding Hope in Serving Community*, Max DePree offers the possibility of a highly collaborative decision-making ethos within the context of a clearly defined hierarchy. Collaborative hierarchy does not happen automatically, in fact, it takes intentionality on the part of the leader, especially when the organization grows. If not addressed, growth can damage a healthy decision-making ethos and undermine collaborative hierarchy. DePree explains that when the company he led grew to 6,000 people, he faced challenges in making sure that the hierarchical structure did not isolate him or his other top leaders from the rest of the company.

In response to this rapid growth, DePree made a decision to nurture a culture of collaboration within the organization. He relates, "My work team and I decided that the six of us would meet once a month over lunch with volunteers from the company."[1] The purpose of the meeting was to experience community and dialogue about issues facing the company. The meetings reflected an intentional effort to make sure that leadership did not become relationally disconnected and marginalize those who were further down the organizational pyramid.

Nurturing of Collaborative Hierarchy in the Congregations Surveyed

Each of the six congregations surveyed for this book experienced significant growth over an extended period of time. Some began as church plants with only a few members and grew to several thousand. Others were small congregations of 100 or 200, steeped in bureaucracy, that have grown into the thousands. In each case, a healthy decision-making ethos did not happen automatically. It had to be nurtured. In some cases the congregation had no decision-making ethos to begin with and had to develop one. In other cases, the congregation had to deconstruct what was in place in order to replace it with something that better positioned the congregation to accomplish its mission. In every case, the growth of the congregation provided challenges. What worked for a congregation of 100 did not necessarily work for a congregation of 4,000. What worked when the congregation was just beginning did not necessarily work when it was larger and more established. While every congregation that was surveyed is unique, some common themes emerged in the nurturing of collaborative hierarchy.

Modeled by the Leader

One of the common themes that emerged was the modeling of collaborative hierarchy by the leader. Each senior pastor tried to find ways to model a healthy environment of collaboration within the staff. One of the core values of Black Rock Congregational Church is making sure that volunteers are included in the collaborative process. Steve Treash talks about the revisiting of that core value that happens each year within the staff, "Every January I gather the whole staff together, and we go over our core values. One of the core values for our staff has to do with respect for our volunteers. We don't want to take advantage of them or use them in an unfair way. We see them as ministry partners and want to encourage them to take leadership by sharing leadership with them."[2]

Treash models this sharing of leadership within his own staff. By including staff in the collaborative process, he demonstrates the way in which he wants staff members to include key ministry leaders in the collaborative process. Treash talks about not wanting his staff to treat key volunteers merely as "grist" in the accomplishment of their own ministry goals. He is careful to make sure that he does not treat the staff in that same fashion. Weekly staff meetings that involve a high level of collaboration are key components in modeling this kind of decision-making ethos.

Harry Kuehl talks about the unhealthy alliances that can develop within staff that undermine collaborative hierarchy, "We have worked hard to prevent alliances from being formed behind the scenes. I have to check myself on this." Kuehl illustrates this with a story about a recent vision-casting meeting for an upcoming worship service. He says, "There was an issue I wanted to go a certain way. I was tempted to call an associate pastor that I knew felt the same way I did, then go into the meeting knowing I had somebody in my corner. But that's not the way we do business. We work hard to prevent those types of alliances from forming."[3]

The Importance of Humility

Each of the senior pastors who were interviewed for this book are strong, assertive leaders who have been able to navigate through the challenges that go with leading a growing congregation. They are willing to make decisions and own those decisions. In fact, they are frustrated by structures that cloud the decision-making process or make unclear who is empowered to make decisions. There is, however, a humility that is apparent in their decision making. Not only are they willing to be collaborative they pursue collaboration. They bring the right people to the table, so they are better positioned to make good decisions. They are not threatened by these additional voices. To the contrary, they highly value them.

Kuehl talks about the importance of senior pastors maintaining a deep relational connectivity with the staff and functioning with a profound sense of humility. He says, "Get to love each other and, above all, maintain a humility that comes from recognizing that Jesus has called the rest of the staff to the church in the same degree as he has called you. God's anointing is over all of you working together as a team. It's not more on one than the other."[4] This sense of humility seems to be at the very center of a healthy collaborative hierarchy.

This profound sense of humility also results in a certain degree of healthy self-evaluation concerning one's own role in the organization. Marty Grubbs talks about the questions that arose in his own mind concerning his leadership abilities in the face of a rapidly growing congregation, "At every level there is no guarantee that I'm the right person for the next level. As a leader, you either learn to lead to the next level, or you have to get out of the way. I've had to keep learning how to lead this growing congregation."[5] Each senior pastor interviewed expressed a similar sentiment concerning the need to change and grow in order to lead effectively and maintain a healthy decision-making ethos in the context of a growing congregation. This fearless self-evaluation does not seem to grow out of an unhealthy sense of doubt but rather out of a burning desire to lead the organization in an increasingly effective fashion.

Empowering the Staff

In his book, *Tribes*, Seth Godin describes a new kind of leadership that is less about managing human resources and more about creating a movement. Godin says, "There's a difference between telling people what to do and inciting a movement. The movement happens when people talk to one another, when ideas spread within the community and most of all, when peer support leads people to do what they always knew was the right thing."[6] Congregations that have experienced sustained growth over a long period of time have developed a decision-making ethos that empowers people to lead. The congregation and the staff sense that they are part of something that really matters, and they have the opportunity to contribute in a significant way. Godin observes, "When you hire amazing people and give them freedom, they do amazing stuff."[7]

If at every level in the organization there are people empowered to lead and their decision making reflects collaborative hierarchy, exciting things begins to happen. This empowerment to lead reduces the fear of making decisions. Mark Batterson says that at National Community Church, "One of our core values is that everything is an experiment. We have a culture where it's okay to make a bad decision. However, we don't want to keep making that bad decision over and over. We want to learn from it, get over it, and keep experimenting." This core value builds some latitude into the decision-making culture of the church so that staff members do not feel paralyzed to make decisions. Batterson continues, "Decisions are made within a cultural context and that culture has a lot do with the kind of decisions you make. For instance, are you making decisions out of fear or are you making decisions because you know risks will actually be rewarded? These are huge factors that are often invisible but influence how decisions get made."[8]

The failure to empower staff can place limits on the ability of a congregation to grow. There was a key moment in the journey of Crossings Community Church where Marty Grubbs realized that a significant change needed to take place in the decision-making ethos of the congregation: "A number of years ago, I realized I had not put strong people around myself. I put people I liked. I put people connected with our movement." The absence of a strong, empowered staff often placed Grubbs in a position that was not beneficial to him or the congregation. He reflects on how this impacted the way some of his staff dealt with conflict, "There would be conflict, and the person in charge would avoid it. So one of the departments would call me. I was like a wasp. I'd fly in, sting, fly off, and head to the next group."[9]

It is extremely difficult to create a healthy decision-making ethos unless the leader is willing to surround himself or herself with people who both understand collaborative hierarchy and function out of it. Not all decisions are popular decisions. One sign of an unhealthy decision-making ethos is when decisions that are made in a collaborative manner are then communicated to others as decisions made in isolation. Grubbs describes the problems created when a staff member functions in this way, "I had a staff person in the past that simply didn't have the courage to communicate tough decisions. He would be a part of the conversation. He would say, 'That's a good idea.' Then he would go to his team and say, 'This is what the senior pastor wants to do.'"[10] This invariably undermines a healthy collaborative hierarchy.

Former U.S. Labor Secretary Robert B. Reich devised a simple, diagnostic tool for measuring the decision-making health of an organization. It involves listening to the pronouns that staff members use when they talk about the organization. He says, "Do employees refer to their company as 'they' or as 'we'? 'They' suggests at least some amount of disengagement, and perhaps even alienation. 'We' suggests the opposite—that employees feel they're part of something significant and meaningful."[11]

The leader of an organization should listen to the way staff members talk about the organization, both in formal and informal settings, to determine if it is a "we" organization or a "they" organization. Pastors of congregations that reflect a healthy decision-making ethos surround themselves with "we" kinds of people rather than "they" kinds of people. In these organizations, staff members are confident that those entrusted with decisions are collaborative in the process and seeking the input of others. When a decision is finally made, they respect the decision and are supportive of it.

Learning from Other Congregations

Another way to nurture a collaborative hierarchy is to develop a collaborative relationship with other organizations and congregations. All of the congregations surveyed were relationally connected to other organizations and congregations and were able to learn from the decision-making ethos of those organizations. Grubbs talks about the importance of regularly connecting with other large congregations: "I take my executive leadership team and we visit with the executive leadership teams of other congregations. We have about an hour and a half sit-down with their team. All of the churches are bigger than ours. Some of them are three or four times bigger. We go to those places because they've been where we are now."[12]

The decision-making ethos of the Church at Rancho Bernardo was influenced by other decision-making structures that the church had not previously been familiar with. Kuehl talks about the impact of taking his staff for the first time to a leadership conference at Willow Creek Community Church, located just outside of Chicago: "I think it's been helpful to look at other congregations, ones that have marks of a healthy, biblically functioning church, and look at the style of leadership that has created that. I'd never really seen the decision-making structure we have now until I went to a leadership conference at Willow Creek."[13]

Each leader, however, was quick to point out that developing a healthy decision-making ethos involved more than just importing another congregation's structure. Treash talks about the process involved in leading Black Rock Congregational Church to a place where the decision-making ethos of the congregation was truly something they could own: "We tend to be very suspicious of other models from other churches in other parts of the country. Some of that is the New England mindset. For that reason, if I try to impose a strategy from somewhere else on my congregation, that is not seen as a victory but as a defeat. Instead, we have to discern our culture and 'cut our own key' for our neighborhood lock."[14]

The common denominator between each of these congregations is the intentionality with which they pursued developing a healthy decision-making ethos. They recognized that health must be constantly modeled, nurtured, and pursued. Sometimes, however, the decision-making ethos of a congregation is so unhealthy that there is little there to nurture. Significant change is required. Chapter 10 deals with the difficult work of changing the decision-making ethos of an established congregation.

Chapter Summary

A healthy decision-making ethos does not happen automatically. It must be intentionally nurtured. Each of the congregations that were the focus of this book found ways to nurture a culture within their organization that produced healthy collaboration. It began with the leader. In each case, the senior pastor modeled collaborative hierarchy in the way that they related to the staff. There is a humility present in their leadership style that not only allows a high level of collaboration to take place but aggressively pursues it. The capacity of the staff to function within the framework and culture of a collaborative hierarchy is equally important. Each pastor talked about the value of hiring the right staff and empowering them to lead. A healthy decision-making ethos rarely develops in isolation. All the pastors interviewed indicated that being able to visit like-minded congregations and talk with the leadership of those congregations helped in developing their own decision-making ethos.

10 | Changing the Decision - Making Ethos of a Church

CHANGING THE DECISION-MAKING ETHOS OF ANY organization is not easy, and that is especially true of local congregations. Denominational systems, formal and informal power structures, and individuals fearful of losing control, all contribute to creating barriers to change. But in many situations, change is desperately needed. An unclear, inefficient, and restrictive decision-making process often limits the potential for kingdom impact. There are many reasons local congregations do not address the issue. The potential for conflict may seem too high, or there may be a naiveté concerning the importance of organizational structure that leads people to minimize its significance. Congregations may believe that any decision-making structure is fine, as long as everyone is well intentioned and functioning in a Christ-like way.

Each of the congregations surveyed for this book are unique congregations, located in unique cities, and are lead by individuals who each have their own unique style. They employ different programming emphases, different worship styles, and different personalities. However, one of the things they all have in common is a commitment to develop a decision-making ethos that empowers leadership, allows for growth, and mobilizes the congregation for mission and ministry. As they reflected on how they were able to affect change in the decision-making ethos of their congregations, several themes emerged.

It Takes Time

Changing the decision-making ethos of a congregation is not a quick process. It usually takes time, especially in more established congregations. Steve Treash has been the senior pastor of Black Rock Congregational Church for thirteen years. He has been on staff for over twenty-three years. He understands that changing the decision-making ethos of the congregation is not something that is accomplished overnight. He says, "It takes patience. I'm convinced it's important to take a long view of change in regards to decision making." For Treash, taking the long view means making sure that the congregation has an understanding of the reason change is needed. He talks about what this involves, "Sometimes you have to talk about change for a long time and get people used to the idea before you make the final decision. Sometimes it may look like you are not being decisive as a leader, but I think it increases the probability that you won't be the only one invested in the change."[1]

Marty Grubbs became the senior pastor of Crossings Community Church is 1985. The rapid growth of the congregation over the past twenty-five years has resulted in several changes in the decision-making structure of the congregation. Grubbs says, "Along the way we've had to ask ourselves is our decision-making structure helping us or is it a hurdle? We found that, generally speaking, the smaller the church, the more decisions that were made by boards and committees. However, the larger the church got, the greater the number of decisions that were being made by staff." Grubbs realized the same thing that many pastors of growing churches come to realize. Committees are generally poor avenues for ministry mobilization. They can actually limit congregational involvement because of a limited number of committee openings, and they often create ambiguity in terms of who is empowered to make decisions. Grubbs reflects on how this has impacted his congregation's organizational structure, "We're constantly getting rid of committees. It's subtle, it's not dramatic, but it continues to evolve. As a leader, you have to be willing to do what needs to be done as you bump into organizational barriers."[2] This evolutionary process of strengthening the decision-making ethos of a congregation takes time.

Not only does it take time to make initial changes to the decision-making ethos of a local congregation, it takes time to establish a new paradigm for how the church and the staff are going to function. Often, changes are made but then, over time, things go back to the way they were before the changes. The decision-making ethos of a congregation often functions like a rubber band. Changes are made, but if the congregation doesn't consistently function over an extended period of time in a way that reflects those changes, eventually it will snap back to the old patterns.

The average tenure for the senior pastors whose congregations were surveyed for this book is nearly twenty-three years. This long-term tenure has not only provided missional consistency, it has provided a visional stability in which lasting change can take place. The change that has taken place in the decision-making ethos of these congregations has not swung back and forth like a pendulum. It has consistently evolved over time. As each congregation grew, structural or systemic barriers were removed that might prevent missional success. The result is a healthy decision-making ethos that allows the organization to focus its energy primarily on making good decisions rather than on dealing with unnecessary conflict over who is empowered to make decisions.

Momentum Helps

It is difficult to implement change in the decision-making ethos of a congregation when the congregation is plateaued or declining. Decision-making structures are even more entrenched when there are not new people coming into the congregation. Power structures are harder to navigate. Treash talks about the importance of missional momentum in being able to effect organizational change,

"I think the number one thing that has allowed us to change has been growth. We needed fresh eyes and fresh hearts related to how we do things." In addition to bringing a new perspective to things, the growth also forced the congregation to look at its structures and systems to see if they were still adequate in light of this much larger congregation. He continues, "We couldn't keep things the way they were. We had to change to deal with the growth."[3] This is often the dilemma a leader faces in trying to change the decision-making ethos of a local congregation. A new decision-making culture is needed in order to reach more people, but an influx of new people is often needed in order to change the decision-making culture.

This is where individuals outside the local congregation can be helpful. Denominational leaders and pastors of sister congregations who have already navigated change in this area can be valuable resources. They can bring a fresh perspective on decision making. Denominational structures, however, vary in terms of the latitude given those outside the congregation to speak into the local context. The initiative often rests in the hands of the congregation. Local congregations that have lost momentum and are in need of addressing decision-making issues would be wise to aggressively pursue outside assistance that is able to help navigate these emotionally charged waters.

Recalibrating Fairfax

Change is difficult, especially in the challenging area of decision making. Motives are often questioned. Trust is tested. Because of this, it is often helpful to get a closer look at how change actually took place in a specific context. It is in that spirit that I began this book with my story at Fairfax Community Church, and it is in the same spirit that I conclude with it. It is not the perfect story, and it is certainly not the only story. It may not even be a very good example of how to affect organizational change in a local congregation. But it is the story I have lived over the past twenty-four years, and it does provide a glimpse of what the process of change can look like in a local congregation.

For the first ten years of my ministry at Fairfax Community Church I functioned with the decision-making ethos I described at the beginning of this book. As a congregation, we made a few small changes to the bylaws, but basically the ethos remained the same. I believed, naively, that the structure didn't really matter. All that mattered was the quality of the relationships within the structure. If those relationships were good, any structure was adequate. I believed that my relationship skills were strong enough that I could effectively lead the church in the direction God desired regardless of the decision-making ethos of the congregation.

By default, our culture of decision making was rooted in consensus building. The goal was to get everyone on board before a final decision was made. The problem with that approach is that God often leads his people into new territory and scary places, and the scarier it gets, the harder it is to reach consensus. Consensus-based decision making tends to bend toward safety and the status quo. A decision-making ethos that relies on reaching a broad consensus before taking action can avoid or postpone difficult decisions.

At the ten-year mark, I was convinced that the decision-making ethos of Fairfax Community Church needed to change. We had experienced healthy growth over the first ten years, but it was becoming increasingly obvious that our kingdom impact would be limited if we did not makes some significant changes. The lay leadership of the congregation agreed. The ethos actually began to change when a couple in our congregation offered to fly me and two of our associate pastors to visit two congregations in Colorado Springs. The couple had just moved from there and had a very high regard for both congregations. I took them up on their gracious offer. I interviewed the senior pastors and staff at both congregations. I learned about their structure and how decisions were made. Neither church had a structure that I wanted to adopt in its entirety, but they opened my eyes to possibilities beyond our current structure.

That experience convinced me that Fairfax Community Church needed a complete redesign of its decision-making ethos, not just a few minor changes. A three-person team, consisting of me and two other members of our Board of Trustees, was formed. We took a blank slate approach to our task. Our goal was not to simply modify our current decision-making structure, but rather to create a structure that empowered leadership, clarified the ownership of decisions, and provided the necessary accountability.

That team met every month for nearly a year. We wanted the process itself to model the structure we were putting into place. As things began to take shape, we would bring drafts of the new structure to the leadership for review and comment. The goal was not to convince or persuade but to present and listen. We would listen to the questions, concerns, and alternate suggestions. We did not defend the new structure; we just listened and took good notes. Then we would go back, reflect on what had been said, incorporate the ideas we believed would make it better, and discard the rest.

We did the same thing with the congregation. We knew, given our current bylaws, the congregation would have to vote to approve this new structure. So we first presented it to the congregation in non-voting environments where they could ask questions and express concerns. Again, we did not defend the new structure. We just listened, clarified, and took good notes. As we had done with the church leadership, we incorporated the ideas we believed would improve the structure and discarded the rest. We had two congregational meetings. For both meetings we brought in denominational and congregational leaders outside of our local congregation to give input and insight. After about a year, the new structure was formally presented and voted on by the congregation. It was overwhelmingly approved.

The detail of the structure is not important for the purpose of this book. However, it is important to say that the structure does provide the context for a healthy decision-making ethos that encourages collaborative hierarchy. The role of our board (we call it the Advisory Council) is clear, there are no standing committees, only the senior pastor reports directly to the board, the staff is empowered to lead, and lines of accountability and ownership of decisions are clear.

In addition, there are two congregational leaders outside of Fairfax Community Church who are included on the eight-member board. The addition of these outside voices has been invaluable to the health and decision-making wisdom of the board. It also gives an additional layer of accountability for the pastor and safety for the congregation since these two members are not under the pastoral leadership of the senior pastor. Our board only meets, in person, three to four times a year. These face-to-face meetings are supplemented by conferences calls, as needed. This reinforces the idea that the board does not have administrative responsibility. Boards that meet more frequently can easily become administrative in focus simply by virtue of how often they come together. Also, all board meetings are designed to include both our inside and outside board members. To do otherwise would undermine the integrity of the board and be unfair to outside members who are fiscally and morally responsible as board members.

The change in the decision-making ethos of Fairfax Community Church has impacted our congregation in so many ways. I am reminded of that every time I walk into our Great Room coffee shop. On most days our collaborative hierarchy is visible as staff members gather to discuss various issues and make decisions. The groups are fluid. Depending upon the issues being addressed, the make-up of the group changes. Those at the table may be staff persons or laypersons. They may represent several levels in the organizational chart. They may all be a part of one department, or they may come from several departments. The result is that the needed expertise on any particular issue is almost always at the table, and yet there is still clarity concerning who owns the decision. The staff members value this collaborative process, and it is reflected in the decisions they make.

If you are a senior pastor, or a staff member of a local congregation, or a congregational leader, you will have to determine the degree to which the Fairfax story relates to your story. There may be lots of similarities, or you may find yourself in a very different context. Either way, you are a part of what I believe is the most important organization in the world. The decisions that are made in the context of that organization have eternal significance. I encourage you to be open to whatever change may be needed in order to develop a decision-making ethos that increases the kingdom impact of your local congregation.

Final Recommendations

The church in America has been entrusted with a tremendous amount of kingdom equity. The value of church buildings and church properties is in the hundreds of billions of dollars. Sadly, much of this kingdom equity is vastly underutilized. It is often tied up in congregations that are plateaued or declining and have lost missional momentum.

In many cases, these congregations are unable to attract visionary leadership. Often, the size of the congregation is seen as the reason. It is argued that these congregations are too small to attract gifted leaders. They don't have the needed resources or personnel to be appealing to a potential pastor. The size of the congregation, however, is generally not the issue. There are an enormous number of gifted young leaders who are willing to invest their lives into starting new congregations where the size of the congregation is effectively zero.

The more important issue, it seems, is the decision-making ethos of the congregation. In many cases, the decision-making ethos of an established congregation is so unhealthy that gifted, visionary leaders avoid the situation. This inability to attract strong leaderships often leads the congregation into a type of death spiral. Congregational consultations or the establishment of congregational task forces rarely change this downward trend. Whatever vision is produced from these short-term efforts is eventually squelched by an unhealthy culture of decision making. In

the unlikely event that a gifted, visionary leader accepts
a call to one of these congregations, the decision-making
ethos of the church often results in a short tenure.

The experience of Bishop Gideon Thompson serves
as a poignant example. Before Thompson started Jubilee
Christian Church in Boston, he pastored another congregation for ten years. It was a wonderful congregation filled
with wonderful people. However, as with so many strong,
vision-oriented pastors, Thompson found the decision-
making ethos of the church to be a hindrance to growth
and missional success. He says, "My position as pastor
was never really respected. Part of it was my age. I went to
a church where everyone was old enough to be my parent.
It was an uphill fight. I just thought if I could make a few
adjustments, things would change. I can't tell you how
many sleepless nights I had and how anxiety producing the
structure of the church was for me."[4]

Many pastors have had a similar experience. They
believe that if they can make a few adjustments to a decision-making ethos that they know is not healthy, they will
be able to achieve the missional success they are convinced
God has called them to. Often, that is not the case. Eventually, the pastor leaves to go to another congregation in the
hopes that the decision-making ethos will be different. In
some cases, they leave vocational ministry altogether. The
result is a vicious cycle of leadership churn. Thompson
reflects on his former congregation, "The church is still in
existence, but they're struggling to survive. They've gone
through a couple of pastors since I left. However, the same

problems exist. They see what the Lord has done at the church I now pastor, and they know it's not just about me. They know it's because we structured ourselves to grow. But it's hard for them to change."[5]

Regrettably, Thompson's experience is not an isolated one. Change the names and the location and this same story is told over and over again. But what would happen if the enormous kingdom equity that lies dormant in so many congregations were to be re-energized? What would happen if a new decision-making ethos could be established in these congregations? What would happen if all of this kingdom equity could be mobilized for radical kingdom activity? What if a larger congregation that already has a healthy decision-making ethos "adopted" a smaller congregation where the culture of decision making may not be so healthy? What if the adopting congregation was willing to pour human and financial resources into the adopted congregation and, in turn, the adopted congregation was to set aside its decision-making structure and functioned under the structure of the adopting church for a season?

It is possible that a new decision-making ethos could emerge that empowered leadership, provided accountability, reflected collaborative hierarchy, and mobilized the church for ministry. It is possible that billions of dollars of kingdom equity could be re-energized and re-invested. It is possible that entire communities could be reengaged with the good news of the kingdom.

What would it take for that to happen? It would take

healthy, growing churches that are willing to invest some of the human and financial resources that God has entrusted to their care. It would take denominational leaders who are willing to "broker the deal," if needed, in order to create an environment of trust. Most importantly, it would take local congregational leaders who are willing to empty themselves of their individual positions of power in order to advance the kingdom. My prayer is that all three would take place and underutilized kingdom equity would once again become available for kingdom impact.

APPENDIX 1

Senior Pastor Interview Questions

1. What changes have taken place during your tenure as senior pastor in the way decisions are made in the congregation?

2. Are most decisions in the congregation entrusted to individuals or groups?

3. How do you foster collaboration among your staff?

4. What struggles/obstacles have you faced in developing an organization that makes good decisions?

5. How does vision formation take place in your congregation?

6. Have there been other congregations/organizations you have looked to in developing your own decision-making ethos?

7. What advice would you give someone trying to develop an organization that makes good decisions?

APPENDIX 2

Survey – Decision Making in Large Churches

All questions to be answered 1 to 5
- 1 indicates that you strongly disagree
- 2 indicates that you disagree
- 3 indicates that you are undecided
- 4 indicates that you agree
- 5 indicates that you strongly agree.

1. There are clear lines of authority in the organization.

2. Staff members who lead departments often consult with their team before making a decision.

3. Staff members are empowered to make decisions in their area of responsibility.

4. Staff members often strategize with other staff members who are outside of their department.

5. Areas of responsibility are clearly defined within the organization.

6. Staff members rarely process decisions with other staff members who are more than one level up or down on the organizational chart.

7. It is clear in the organization who is responsible for what decisions.

8. Staff members often seek guidance in making deci-

sions from persons who have expertise in a particular area regardless of the person's position in the organization.

9. It is clearly understood within the organization who is responsible for hiring and firing staff.

10. The decision to hire/fire a particular staff member is usually made by one person without the consultation of others.

11. Each staff department has a clearly designated leader.

12. Staff members are empowered to bring whoever is needed into the discussion in order to make a good decision.

13. Most decisions in the organization are entrusted to individuals rather than groups.

14. Staff members often process decisions with lay people in the congregation.

15. The organization has a chart clearly identifying each staff position and who they report to.

16. Some staff members report to both another staff member and a committee/board.

17. Each staff member within the organization is easily accessible to other staff members regardless of position.

18. If approval is needed for a particular decision, staff members know who to ask for approval.

19. Titles are very important within the organization.

20. Conflict sometimes arises over what group or individual is empowered to make a decision.

21. Staff members tend to ask lots of questions before making a decision.

22. Decisions that require congregational approval are clearly understood.

23. Persons with expertise in a particular area can influence decisions regardless of their position in the organization.

24. Decisions that require the approval of the governing board are clearly understood.

25. The make-up of who is invited into the discussion may change depending upon the decision being made.

26. Most staff members can clearly communicate their area of responsibility in a sentence or two.

APPENDIX 3

Respondent Data by Gender

Respondent	Gender	Hierarchy	Collaborative
1	Male	3	3.58
2	Male	3.07	3.75
3	Male	3.36	4.08
4	Male	4	3.42
5	Male	3.21	3.83
6	Male	3.43	2.58
7	Male	3.86	3.83
8	Male	4.21	3.75
9	Male	4.36	3.83
10	Male	4.21	3.92
11	Male	3.58	3.5
12	Male	3.36	2.08
13	Male	3.86	3.58
14	Male	4.29	3.75
15	Male	4.43	4.25
16	Male	3.43	2.67
17	Male	4.14	3.58
18	Male	3.86	3.83
19	Male	4.36	4.5
20	Male	4.64	4
21	Male	4.36	3.67
22	Male	4.5	4.33
23	Male	4.43	3.67
24	Male	3.71	3.73
25	Male	3.93	4.17
26	Male	4.07	4.25

27	Male	3.79	4.17
28	Male	4.57	4.5
29	Male	3.93	4.08
30	Male	3.57	3.17
31	Male	3.71	3.67
32	Male	4.57	4.7
33	Male	3.64	3.92
34	Male	3.57	4.17
35	Male	3.37	3.67
36	Male	3.79	3.58
37	Male	4	3.67
38	Male	3.07	3.33
39	Male	3.43	3.42
Average Male Data		*3.86*	*3.75*

Respondent	Gender	Hierarchy	Collaborative
40	Female	4.21	4.58
41	Female	4.79	4.08
42	Female	3.64	4.33
43	Female	3.57	3.5
44	Female	3.57	3.67
45	Female	5	4.25
46	Female	3.76	2.75
47	Female	3.43	3.67
48	Female	3	4.3
49	Female	4.43	3.92
50	Female	4.71	4.75
51	Female	3.86	2.75
52	Female	3.79	3.75
53	Female	3.79	3.67

54	Female	3.86	4.08
55	Female	3.21	3.17
56	Female	3.71	3.67
57	Female	4.07	3.75
58	Female	4	3.33
59	Female	3.5	3.67
60	Female	3.86	4.17
61	Female	3.64	4.18
62	Female	3.57	3.5
63	Female	3.86	3.58
64	Female	4.14	4.17
65	Female	4.43	3.75
66	Female	3.64	3.17
67	Female	3.93	3.64
68	Female	4	3.42
69	Female	3.71	3.67
70	Female	3.79	4.17
71	Female	3.79	3.25
72	Female	3	2.17
73	Female	2.57	2.5
Average Female Data		*3.82*	*3.68*

APPENDIX 4

Respondent Data by Age

Respondent	Age	Hierarchy	Collaborative
1	20-29	3	3.58
2	20-29	3.07	3.75
3	20-29	3.36	4.08
4	20-29	3.57	3.67
5	20-29	4.14	3.58
6	20-29	4.07	3.75
7	20-29	4.5	4.33
8	20-29	3.5	3.67
9	20-29	3.71	3.67
10	20-29	3.79	3.25
11	20-29	3	2.17
Average 20-29 Data		*3.61*	*3.59*

Respondent	Age	Hierarchy	Collaborative
12	30-39	4	3.42
13	30-39	4.21	4.58
14	30-39	3.57	3.5
15	30-39	3.21	3.83
16	30-39	3.86	3.83
17	30-39	3	4.3
18	30-39	3.58	3.5
19	30-39	3.86	3.58
20	30-39	4.29	3.75
21	30-39	4.43	4.25

22	30-39	3.43	2.67
23	30-39	3.86	3.83
24	30-39	4.07	4.25
25	30-39	3.57	3.5
26	30-39	3.86	3.58
27	30-39	3.57	3.17
28	30-39	3.37	3.67
29	30-39	3.79	3.58
30	30-39	4	3.67
31	30-39	3.79	4.17
Average 30-39 Data		*3.77*	*3.73*

Respondent	Age	Hierarchy	Collaborative
32	40-49	4.79	4.08
33	40-49	3.64	4.33
34	40-49	3.76	2.75
35	40-49	3.43	2.58
36	40-49	3.43	3.67
37	40-49	4.43	3.92
38	40-49	4.36	3.83
39	40-49	3.36	2.08
40	40-49	3.79	3.75
41	40-49	3.79	3.67
42	40-49	3.86	4.08
43	40-49	3.71	3.67
44	40-49	4.64	4
45	40-49	4	3.33
46	40-49	4.43	3.67
47	40-49	3.86	4.17
48	40-49	4.57	4.5

49	40-49	3.64	3.17
50	40-49	3.93	3.64
51	40-49	3.93	4.08
52	40-49	4	3.42
53	40-49	3.57	4.17
54	40-49	2.57	2.5
Average 40-49 Data		*3.89*	*3.61*

Respondent	Age	Hierarchy	Collaborative
55	50+	5	4.25
56	50+	4.21	3.75
57	50+	4.21	3.92
58	50+	4.71	4.75
59	50+	3.86	2.75
60	50+	3.21	3.17
61	50+	4.36	4.5
62	50+	4.36	3.67
63	50+	3.71	3.73
64	50+	3.64	4.18
65	50+	3.93	4.17
66	50+	4.14	4.17
67	50+	3.79	4.17
68	50+	4.43	3.75
69	50+	3.71	3.67
70	50+	4.57	4.7
71	50+	3.64	3.92
72	50+	3.43	3.42
Average 50+ Data		*4.05*	*3.92*

ENDNOTES

Chapter 1

1 David T. Olsen, The American Church in Crisis (Grand Rapids, MI: Zondervan, 2008), 28.

2 Ibid., 34.

3 Ibid., 175.

4 Shauna L. Anderson et al., "Dearly Departed: How Often Do Congregations Close?" Journal for the Scientific Study of Religion 47, no. 2 (June 1, 2008): 326.

5 Ibid., 327.

6 Ibid.

7 Olsen, 16.

8 Frank Hobbs and Nicole Stoops, U.S. Census Bureau, Census 2000 Special Reports, Series CENSR-4, "Demographic Trends in the 20th Century," U.S. Government Printing Office, http://www.census.gov/prod/2002pubs/censr-4.pdf (accessed January 15, 2008), 9.

9 Ibid., 7.

10 Ibid., 9.

11 Ibid., 34.

12 Ibid., 37.

13 Eduardo Lopez and Rasna Warah, "The State of the World's Cities Report, Urban and Slum Trends in the 21st Century," The Free Library, http://www.thefreelibrary.com/The+State+of+the+World%27s+Cities+Report+2006%2f7%3a+Urban+and+slum+trends+...-a0152633371 (accessed March 14, 2011).

14 Tim Keller, "What is God's Global Urban Mission?" Cape Town 2010 Advance Paper, (May 18, 2010), http://conversation.lausanne.org/en/conversations/detail/10282#article_page_4 (accessed November 14, 2010).

15 Ibid.

16 Ibid.

17 Scott Thumma, Dave Travis and Warren Bird, "Megachurches Today 2005: Summary of Research Findings," Hartford Institute for Religion Research, http://hirr.hartsem.edu/megachurch/megastoday2005_summaryreport.html (accessed January 16, 2008).

18 Ibid.

19 Scott Thumma and Dave Travis, Beyond Megachurch Myths: What We Can Learn from America's Largest Churches (San Francisco: Jossey-Bass, 2007), 1.

20 Ibid., 175.

21 Ibid., 176.

22 Ibid., 183.

Chapter 2

1 The term "senior pastor" will be used throughout the project, even though in some cases the congregation may use other terms such as "lead pastor" or "bishop" to describe the position.

2 Steve Treash, interview by author, Fairfax, VA, October 12, 2010.

3 Black Rock Congregational Church, "About BRCC," Black Rock Congregational Church. http://www.brcc.org/about/about.html (accessed November 20, 2010).

4 National Community Church, "About NCC," National Community Church. http://theaterchurch.com/about (accessed November 5, 2010).

5 Harry Kuehl, interview by author, Fairfax, VA, October 6, 2010.

6 1985 Yearbook of the Church of God, (Anderson, IN: Executive Council of the Church of God, Division of Church Service) 1985.

7 2010 Yearbook of the Church of God, (Anderson, IN: Warner Press, Inc.) 2010.

8 2011 Yearbook of the Church of God, (Anderson, IN: Warner Press, Inc.) 2011.

Chapter 3

1 Mark Batterson, interview by author, Fairfax VA, September 28, 2010.

2 Ibid.

3 Marty Grubbs, interview by author, Fairfax, VA, September 28, 2010.

4 Gideon Thompson, interview by author, Fairfax, VA, November 2, 2010.

5 Ibid.

6 Kuehl interview.

7 Ibid.

8 Ibid.

9 John Carver and Miriam Carver, "Carver's Policy Governance Model in Nonprofit Organizations ," Policy Governance.com, http://www.carvergovernance.com/pg-np.htm (accessed November 11, 2010).

10 Ibid.

11 Ibid.

12 Ibid.

13 Ibid.

14 Ibid.

15 Ibid.

16 Ibid.

17 Eph. 4:12 (NIV). All scripture references are from the New International Version (NIV) of the Bible.

18 Heb. 13:17.

19 1 Pet. 2:24-25.

20 Acts 20:28.

21 1 Tim. 3:1-7.

22 1 Pet. 5:1-4.

Chapter 4

1 Treash interview.

2 Kuehl interview.

3 Batterson interview.

4 Ibid.

5 Susan Willhauck and Jacqulyn Thorpe, The Web of Women's Leadership: Recasting Congregational Ministry (Nashville: Abingdon Press, 2001), 30.

6 Ibid., 22.

7 Josh Packard, "Organizational Structure, Religious Belief, and Resistance: The Emerging Church" (PhD diss.,Vanderbilt University, 2008), 114.

8 Ibid., 148.

9 Gilbert Bilezikian, Community 101: Reclaiming the Local Church as Community of Oneness, (Grand Rapids, MI: Zondervan Publishing House, 1997), 24.

10 Ibid., 26.

11 Greg Ogden, The New Reformation – Returning the Ministry to the People of God (Grand Rapids, MI: Zondervan Publishing House, 1990), 51.

12 Ibid.

13 Ibid., 52.

14 Ori Brafman and Rod A. Beckstrom, The Starfish and the Spider: The Unstoppable Power of Leaderless Organizations (NY: Penguin Group, 2006), 36, Ipad iBook.

15 Ibid., 37-38.

16 Ibid., 22.

17 Ibid., 148-149.

18 Ibid.

19 Ibid., 39-40.

20 Ibid.

21 Ibid., 42.

Chapter 5

1 Bilezikian, 150.

2 Ogden, 142.

3 Ibid., 180.

4 Ibid., 176.

5 Brafman and Beckstrom, 149-150.

6 Patrick Nachtigall, Mosaic: A Journey Across the Church of God (Anderson, IN: Warner Press, 2010), 267.

7 N.J. Demerath III et al., Sacred Companies - Organizational Aspects of Religion and Religious Aspects of Organization, (NY: Oxford University Press, 1998), 11.

8 Thompson interview.

9 Batterson interview.

10 Grubbs interview.

11 Ron Ashkenas et al., The Boundaryless Organization: Breaking the Chains of Organization Structure, Revised and Updated, 2nd ed., rev. & upd. (San Francisco, CA.: Jossey-Bass, 2002), 2.

12 Ibid.

13 Ibid., 3.

14 Ibid., 3-4.

15 Bill Gaither, "The Family of God," Benson Sound, MP3 file, http://www.bensonsound.com/lyrics/0371.htm (accessed August 11, 2008).

16 Max DePree, Leading Without Power: Finding Hope in Serving Community (San Francisco: Jossey-Bass, 1997), 90.

17 Ibid., 91-94.

18 Ibid., 166.

Chapter 6

1 Prov. 15:22.

2 Acts 15:1.

3 Acts 15:5.

4 Acts 15:7b-11.

5 Acts 15:12.

6 Acts 15:19-20.

7 Acts 15:28-29a.

8 Acts 15:30-31.

9 Luke Timothy Johnson, Scripture and Discernment—Decision Making in The Church (Nashville: Abingdon Press, 1983), 88.

10 Gal. 2:2.

11 Gal. 2:9-10.

12 Exod. 18:17b-19a.

13 Exod. 18:22a.

14 Exod. 18:24.

15 Num. 10:13b.

16 Num. 10:31-32.

17 Num. 32:2, 4-5.

18 Num. 32:20a, 21-22.

19 Josh. 17:4a.

20 Josh. 17:4b.

21 Num. 13:33b.

22 Num. 13:30.

23 Ezek. 7:27.

24 Ezek. 7:26b.

Chapter 7

1 Num. 12:2.

2 Num. 12:6-8.

3 Acts 2:2-4.

4 Acts 2:17-18.

5 Acts 2:36b-38.

6 Acts 2:42, 46.

7 Acts 2:47.

8 Batterson interview.

9 Geoff Surratt, Greg Ligon and Warren Bird, Multisite Church Roadtrip: Exploring the New Normal (Grand Rapids, MI: Zondervan, 2009), 217.

10 Kuehl interview.

11 Ibid.

12 Ibid.

13 Treash interview.

14 Ibid.

15 Thompson interview.

16 Ibid.

17 Ibid.

Chapter 8

1 Ashish Nanda, "The Risky Business of Hiring Stars" (lecture, Willow Creek Association Leadership Summit, South Barrington, IL, August 11, 2006).

2 Eddie Gibbs, Leadership Next: Changing Leaders in a Changing World (Downers Grove, IL: InterVarsity Press, 2005), 25.

3 Ibid., 13.

4 Stephen A. Rhodes, Where the Nations Meet: The Church in a Multicultural World (Downers Grove, IL: InterVarsity Press, 1998), 114.

5 Jim Collins, How the Mighty Fall: And Why Some Companies Never Give In (London: Random House Business Books, 2009), 20-22.

6 Batterson interview.

7 2 Chron. 25:7-8.

Chapter 9

1 DePree, 58.

2 Treash interview.

3 Kuehl interview.

4 Ibid.

5 Grubbs interview.

6 Seth Godin, Tribes: We Need You to Lead Us (NY: Penguin Group, 2008), 30, Ipad iBook.

7 Ibid., 100.

8 Batterson interview.

9 Grubbs interview.

10 Ibid.

11 Daniel Pink, Drive: The Surprising Truth About What Moti-

vates Us (NY: Riverhead Books, 2009), 132, Ipad iBook.

12 Grubbs interview.

13 Kuehl interview.

14 Treash interview.

Chapter 10

1 Treash interview.

2 Grubbs interview.

3 Treash interview.

4 Thompson interview.

5 Ibid.

BIBLIOGRAPHY

Ammerman, Nancy T., Jackson W. Carroll, Carl S. Dudley, and William McKinney. *Studying Congregations: A New Handbook.* Nashville, TN: Abingdon Press, 1998.

Anderson, Keith R., and Randy D. Reese. *Spiritual Mentoring—A Guide for Seeking and Giving Direction.* Downers Grove, IL: Inter-Varsity Press, 1999.

Anderson, Shauna L., Jessica Hamar Martinez, Catherine Hoegeman, Gary Adler and Mark Chaves. "Dearly Departed: How Often Do Congregations Close?" *Journal for the Scientific Study of Religion* 47, no. 2 (June 1, 2008): 321-328.

Ashkenas, Ron, Dave Ulrich, Todd Jick, and Steve Kerr. *The Boundaryless Organization: Breaking the Chains of Organization Structure.* 2nd ed., Rev. Upd. San Francisco, California: Jossey-Bass, 2002.

Auletta, Ken. Googled: *The End of the World as We Know It.* NY: The Penguin Press, 2009. Ipad iBook.

Baron, David, and Lynette Padwa. *Moses on Management: 50 Leadership Lessons from the Greatest Manager of All Time.* NY: Pocket Books, 1999. Ipad iBook.

Belcher, Jim. *Deep Church: A Third Way Beyond Emerging and Traditional.* Downers Grove, IL: InterVarsity Press, 2009. Ipad Kindle.

Bilezikian, Gilbert. *Community 101: Reclaiming the Local Church as Community of Oneness.* Grand Rapids, MI: Zondervan Publishing House, 1997.

Black Rock Congregational Church. "About BRCC." Black Rock Congregational Church. http://www.brcc.org/about/about.html (accessed November 20, 2010).

Brace, Ian. *Questionnaire Design: How to Plan, Structure*

and Write Survey Material for Effective Market Research. London: Kogan Page Ltd., 2005.

Brafman, Ori, and Rod A. Beckstrom. *The Starfish and the Spider: The Unstoppable Power of Leaderless Organizations*. NY: Penguin Group, 2006. Ipad iBook.

Brown, Jim. *The Imperfect Board Member: Discovering the Seven Principles of Governance Excellence*. San Francisco, CA: Jossey-Bass, 2006.

Buckingham, Marcus. *Go Put Your Strengths to Work: Six Powerful Steps to Achieve Outstanding Performance*. NY: Simon and Schuster, 2007.

Buffett, Mary, and David Clark. *Warren Buffett's Management Secrets: Proven Tools for Personal and Business Success*. NY: Scribner, 2009. Ipad iBook.

Carnegie, Dale. *Leadership Mastery: How to Challenge Yourself and Others to Greatness*. NY: Simon And Schuster, Inc., 2000. Ipad iBook.

Carver, John, and Miriam Carver. "Carver's Policy Governance® Model in Nonprofit Organizations." PolicyGovernance.com. http://www.carvergovernance.com/pg-np.htm (accessed November 11, 2010).

Collins, James C. *Good to Great: Why Some Companies Make the Leap . . . and Others Don't*. NY: HarperCollins Publishing, 2001.

------. *Good to Great and the Social Sectors: Why Business Thinking Is Not the Answer : a Monograph to Accompany Good to Great : Why Some Companies Make the Leap--and Others Don't*. Boulder, CO: J. Collins, 2005.

------. *How The Mighty Fall – And Why Some Companies Never Give In*., London: Random House Business Books, 2009.

Collins, James C., and Jerry I. Porras. *Built to Last: Successful Habits of Visionary Companies*. NY: HarperBusiness, 1994.

Covey, Stephen M.R., and Rebecca R. Merrill. *The Speed of Trust: The One Thing That Changes Everything*. NY: Free Press, 2006.

Culbert Samuel A. *Get Rid of the Performance Review!: How Companies Can Stop Intimidating, Start Managing—and Focus on What Really Matters*. NY: Hachette Book Group, 2010. Ipad iBook.

Demerath N.J. III, Peter Dobkin Hall, Terry Schmitt and Rhys H. William. *Sacred Companies - Organizational Aspects of Religion and Religious Aspects of Organizations*. NY: Oxford University Press, 1998.

DePree, Max. *Leading Without Power: Finding Hope in Serving Community*. San Francisco, CA: Jossey-Bass, 1997.

Diehl, William E. *Ministry in Daily Life—A Practical Guide for Congregations*. Herndon, VA: The Alban Institute, 2001.

Eck, Diana L. *A New Religious America: How a "Christian Country" Has Become the World's Most Religiously Diverse Nation*. NY: HarperCollins Publishers, Inc., 2002.

Ford, Kevin. *Transforming Church: Bringing Out the Good to Get to the Great*. Carol Stream, IL: Tyndale House Publishers, Inc., 2007.

Gaither, Bill. "The Family of God." Benson Sound. MP3 file. http://www.bensonsound.com/lyrics/0371.htm (accessed August 11, 2008).

Gibbs, Eddie. *Leadership Next: Changing Leaders in a Changing World*. Downers Grove, IL: InterVarsity Press, 2005.

Gibbs, Eddie, and Ian Coffey. *Church Next: Quantum Changes in How We Do Ministry*. Downers Grove, IL: InterVarsity Press, 2000.

Godin, Seth. Tribes: *We Need You to Lead Us*. NY: Penguin Group, 2008. Ipad iBook.

Greenway, Roger S., and Timothy M. Monsma. Cities: Missions' New Frontier. Grand Rapids, MI: Baker Books, 2000.

Hamel, Gary, and Bill Breen. *The Future of Management*. Boston, MA: Harvard Business School Press, 2007.Hellerman, Joseph H. *When the Church Was a Family: Recapturing Jesus' Vision for Authentic Christian Community*. Nashville, TN: B & H Academic, 2009.

-------. The Ancient Church As Family. Minneapolis, MN: Fortress Press, 2001.

Hitchcock, Jeff. *Lifting the White Veil: An Exploration of White American Culture in a Multiracial Context*. Roselle, NJ: Crandall, Dostie & Douglass Books, Inc., 2002.

Hobbs, Frank, and Nicole Stoops. U.S. Census Bureau, Census 2000 Special Reports, Series CENSR-4, "Demographic Trends in the 20th Century." U.S. Government Printing Office. http://www.census. gov/prod/2002pubs/censr-4.pdf (accessed January 15, 2008).

Hunter, George G. *Leading and Managing a Growing Church*. Nashville, TN: Abingdon Press, 2000.

Hybels, Bill. *Courageous Leadership*. Grand Rapids, MI: Zondervan, 2002.

Jacobs, Charles S. *Management Rewired, Why Feedback Doesn't Work and Other Surprising Lessons from the Latest Brain Science*. NY: The Penguin Group, 2009. Ipad iBook.

Johnson, Luke Timothy. *Scripture and Discernment— Decision Making in the Church*. Nashville, TN: Abingdon Press, 1983.

Keller, Tim. "Ministry Movements." Redeemer City to City. Entry posted June 27, 2010. http://redeemercitytocity.com/blog/view.jsp?Blog_param=203 (accessed February 3, 2011).

-------. "What is God's Global Urban Mission?" Cape Town 2010 Advance Paper. http://conversation.lausanne. org/en/conversations/detail/10282#article_page_4 (accessed November 14, 2010).

Lencioni, Patrick. *The Five Dysfunctions of a Team: A Leadership Fable.* San Francisco, CA: Jossey-Bass, 2002.

Lederach, John Paul. *The Little Book of Conflict Transformation.* Intercourse, PA: Good Books, 2003.

Lopez, Eduardo, and Rasna Warah. "The State of the World's Cities Report, Urban and Slum Trends in the 21st Century," The Free Library. http://www. thefreelibrary.com/The+State+of+the+World%27 s+Cities+Report+2006%2f7%3a+Urban+and+slu m+trends+...-a0152633371 (accessed March 14, 2011).

March, James G., and Chip Heath, *A Primer on Decision Making: How Decisions Happen.* NY: Simon and Schuster, 1994. Ipad iBook.

McManus, Erwin Raphael. *An Unstoppable Force: Daring to Become the Church God Had in Mind.* Loveland, CO: Group Publishing, 2001.

Nachtigall, Patrick. *Mosaic: A Journey Across the Church of God.* Anderson, IN: Warner Press, 2010.

Nanda, Ashish. "The Risky Business of Hiring Stars." Lecture, Willow Creek Association Leadership Summit, South Barrington, IL, August 11, 2006.

National Community Church. "About NCC." National Community Church. http://theaterchurch.com/ about (accessed November 5, 2010).

Ogden, Greg. *The New Reformation – Returning the Ministry to the People of God.* Grand Rapids, MI: Zondervan Publishing House, 1990.

Olsen, David T. *The American Church in Crisis.* Grand Rapids, MI: Zondervan, 2008.

Packard, Josh. *Organizational Structure, Religious Belief, and Resistance: The Emerging Church.* PhD. diss., Vanderbilt University, 2008.

Pink, Daniel. *Drive: The Surprising Truth About What Motivates Us.* NY: Riverhead Books, 2009. Ipad iBook.

Rainer, Thom S. *Breakout Churches: Discover How to Make the Leap.* Grand Rapids, MI: Zondervan, 2005. Ipad iBook.

Rainer, Thom, and Eric Geiger. *Simple Church: Returning to God's Process For Making Disciples.* Nashville, Tennessee: B&H Publishing Group, 2006.

Rhodes, Stephen A. *Where the Nations Meet: The Church in a Multicultural World.* Downers Grove, IL: InterVarsity Press, 1998.

Scazzero, Peter, and Warren Bird. *The Emotionally Healthy Church: A Strategy for Discipleship That Actually Changes Lives.* Grand Rapids, MI: Zondervan, 2003. Ipad iBook.

Schaller, Lyle E. *The Very Large Church: New Rules for Leaders.* Nashville, TN: Abingdon Press, 2000.

Schwarz, Christian A. *Paradigm Shift in the Church: How Natural Church Development Can Transform Theological Thinking.* Carol Stream, IL: ChurchSmart Resources, 1999.

------. *The ABC's of Natural Church Development.* translated by Erich Rick Baumgartner. Carol Stream, IL: ChurchSmart Resources, 1998.

Schwarz, Christian A., and Christoph Schalk. *Implementation Guide To Natural Church Development.* St. Charles, IL: ChurchSmart Resources, 1998.

Slocum, Robert. *Maximizing Your Ministry.* Colorado Springs, CO: Navpress, 1990.

Stetzer, Ed, and Thom S. Rainer. *Transformational Church: Creating a New Scorecard for Congregations*. Nashville, TN: B&H Publishing Group, 2010. Ipad iBook.

Stevens, Mark. *Extreme Management: What They Teach at Harvard Business School's Advanced Management Program*. NY: Warner Books Inc., 2001. Ipad iBook.

Stevens, R. Paul. *The Equipper's Guide to Every-Member Ministry: Eight Ways Ordinary People Can Do the Work of the Church*. Vancouver, B.C.: Regent College Publishing, 2000.

Surratt, Geoff, Greg Ligon and Warren Bird. *Multisite Church Roadtrip: Exploring the New Normal*. Grand Rapids, MI: Zondervan, 2009.

Swanson, Eric, and Sam Williams. *To Transform a City: Whole Church Whole Gospel Whole City*. Grand Rapids, MI: Zondervan, 2010. Ipad iBook.

Thumma, Scott, and Dave Travis. *Beyond Megachurch Myths: What We Can Learn from America's Largest Churches*. San Francisco, CA: Jossey-Bass, 2007.

Thumma, Scott, Dave Travis and Warren Bird. "Megachurches Today 2005: Summary of Research Findings," Hartford Institute for Religion Research. *http://hirr.hartsem.edu/megachurch/megastoday2005_summaryreport.html* (accessed January 16, 2008).

Tolbert, Bill, with Susanne Cook-Greuter, Dalmer Fisher, Erica Foldy, Alain Gauthier, Jackie Keeley, David Rooke, Sara Ross, Catherine Royce, Jenny Rudolph, Steve Taylor, and Mariana Tran. *Action Inquiry: The Secret of Timely and Transforming Leadership*, San Francisco, CA: Berrett-Koehler Publishers, Inc. 2004. Ipad Kindle.

Wheatley, Margaret J. *Leadership and the New Science: Discovering Order in a Chaotic World*. San Francisco, CA: Berrett-Koehler Publishers, Inc., 2006. Ipad Kindle.

Wilkes, Paul. *Excellent Protestant Congregations: The Guide to Best Places and Practices*. Louisville, KY: Westminster John Knox Press, 2001.

Willhauck, Susan, and Jacqulyn Thorpe. *The Web of Women's Leadership: Recasting Congregational Ministry*. Nashville, TN: Abingdon Press, 2001.

Made in United States
North Haven, CT
27 January 2022

15347234R00122